Way of the Wealthy

In the Footsteps of the Masters

7 FINANCIAL LAWS AND UNIVERSAL PRINCIPLES THAT WILL TRANSFORM YOUR LIFE

By John Hanna
&
Timothy Marlowe

Way
of the
Wealthy

In the Footsteps of the Masters

7 Financial Laws and 7 Universal Principles
That Will Transform Your Life

By John Hanna
&
Timothy Marlowe

"A fantastic read full of inspirational stories. It blends beautifully the practical with the theoretical, and this book of universal truths will take you on a trip from the physical to the metaphysical and back. It's compelling and thought-provoking, and cannot help but make you take action! You too can stand on the shoulders of giants."
~ Arthur Panagis ~ Financial Strategist

"At a time when things seemed the most hopeless, 'Way of the Wealthy' showed me that I could not only turn my life around, but that I deserved to have it happen. Since reading the book my finances continue to improve and, for the first time in a long time, I'm excited about what's to come. This is one of the best-written books I've ever read, and I've read a lot of books."
~ Anthony Vercoe ~ University Lecturer and Screenwriter

"I loved 'Way of the Wealthy' for so many reasons – its practical and easy to follow advice, its touching stories, its spiritual essence, its inspirational content, as well as being a great read. I don't think there is another financial advice book quite like this one… Tim and John have created something wonderfully unique."
~ Gillian Anderson ~ Government Project Director and Consultant

"This book highlighted the disempowering stories I had been telling myself for years, and also showed me why I create great wealth but haven't been able to hold onto it. Within 2 months of rereading this book I'm more than halfway through my first 'base' in the savings pyramid, and will own my own home in 2 years. I found my property this week, and know the means to make it mine will flow faster than ever before. Your book has turned my life around in so many ways, and above all made me realise my own value. I will pass it on as a gift. Thank you so much."
~ Dr Annica Larsdotter ~

"This book is a master class in Wealth Creation. Its thoughtful approach makes the profound insights and strategies accessible and useful to anyone from novice to seasoned financial expert. The wisdom I found here

has guided me to a place I never thought I could reach. In fact, I stayed up all night reading it, went in the next morning and quit my boring job, and am now doing what truly inspires me. Thank you so much."
~ Daniel Richard Montana ~ Film Producer, Annie B Productions

"Your book brought me to tears this morning. 'Way of the Wealthy' gives exquisite clarity on applying universal laws to acquiring wealth and transforming one's life. I feel as if it was written for me personally, and it moved me deeply with a crystal clear reminder to honour and act on my highest values. The 'voice' of this book is kind, real, compassionate, precise, and empowering. I'll be ordering more copies as gifts to my children and many others. I LOVE YOUR BOOK."
~ Liliane Grace ~ author of The Mastery Club and The Hidden Order

"Thanks so much for your book. I couldn't put it down and finished in record time. You present esoteric principles in a way that makes them so clear and compelling, and inspired me to be disciplined in building my wealth. I love your explanation of the power of compound interest, and now I finally understand leveraging. This book is a gem. Thanks again."
~ Vicki Kilias ~ Physicist

"Thanks for a great book, it makes universal laws so clear to the uninitiated, and plants the seeds for future transformation. I'm not a big feeler, but I was teary-eyed at several points. I'm inspired about managing our finances on a higher level with the deeper understanding, love and appreciation I now have. I'm just waiting for my wife to finish the book so I can reread it, a real measure of its appeal as she rarely reads what I do. What is your next book?"
~ Leonard Hight ~ Systems Analyst

" 'Way of the Wealthy' is truly inspirational, and accessible to everyone from wealth-seekers to those who want to increase the wealth they already have. It offers many strategies to transform finances at every level, and I loved the wonderful quotes."
~ Sofia Smithers ~ Composer, Ultimate Film and Television Music

For information contact:
John Hanna and Timothy Marlowe

Suite 323, Level 3,
5 Lime Street,
Sydney, NSW, 2000
Australia

Published by John Hanna and Timothy Marlowe

Cover design and layout by Désirée DeKlerk
desiree.news@gmail.com

First Edition 2012

Printed in Australia

Contents

Foreword

This book is about wealth and how to create it. If you sincerely follow these simple principles, your life is about to change. You may have heard that before and been disappointed, because there are vast numbers of teachers and books on wealth creation making the same claims that exercise products do – that is, the results will be effortless, immediate, and you won't have to change or work or even think very much to get them. We all know that's nonsense, playing on our hopes and fears, but it just seems so *irresistible*. So we try, but the books end up on the shelf and the magical exercise machine gathers dust in the garage, and all that changes is our courage, and our belief that we deserve more.

So what makes this book any different? Three things. First of all, we knew that if it was just another dense mass of financial charts, investment projections, and other incomprehensible data, those who need it wouldn't read it, and those who knew it wouldn't need it. If it isn't clear, people won't do it, and neither would we. So we didn't write that book.

Secondly, we appreciate that the single most important factor in any real and lasting transformation is… you. If *you* don't change, all the knowledge in the world won't change your life, so we address both; not only the practical steps that will increase your wealth no matter what level you're at now, but also principles and exercises that will have a profound effect on who you are and what you feel you deserve from the world – the doing *and* the being. This is not a book you read, but a book you *live*.

Finally, this knowledge does not come from us alone. It is the result of over 70 combined years of diligent research and personal experience, with the guidance of all the inspired masters of the past and present we have been privileged to learn from, meet, or work with. This wisdom has stood the test of time, has proven its value, and it is deeply satisfying to help others gain quickly what took us so long to learn. Albert Einstein said, "If I see far, it is because I stand upon the shoulders of giants," and so do we.

It's not enough just to make money, although we'll certainly teach you how to do that. Even more important is learning how to *keep* it, to *grow* it, and *use* it to create a magnificent life. There are two primary aspects to life; the tangible, material things of this world, and the intangible spiritual essence that permeates it all. Those who pursue only the material find that no matter how successful they become there is always something missing, some gap that no amount of wealth or possessions can fill. On the other hand, those who attempt to follow a path of pure spirit find themselves continually challenged and brought back down to earth by the practical demands of existence – and they also miss out on much of the beauty and opportunities this world has to offer, because they simply can't afford it.

Financial laws are the principles by which wealth operates and is governed, universal principes are the laws by which the universe is run on every level. In order to create a truly whole life, it is necessary to honour both spirit and matter. We know this is true from personal experience. We've each tried to live one side of life, and have been irresistibly compelled to embrace the other because either side alone is only half the story, and can never be more than 'half-fillment'. Genuine fulfillment only comes from honouring and mastering both aspects of our existence.

We will be revealing the secrets behind 7 Financial Laws and 7 Universal Principles which will make this possible. That is our promise to you.

Shall we begin?

Acknowledgments

We would like to thank these masters for their guidance on the Way, each in their own field of expertise.

Dr John F. Demartini ~ Mentor, colleague, and friend, whose profound philosophy formed the nucleus of this book, particularly his work on Values and the power of Inspiration.

Sogyal Rinpoche, Tibetan Lama ~ Thank you for the 'Transmission of the Nature of Mind'.

Robert Kiyosaki ~ He showed me that life is a game to be played with 100% responsibility for everything that happens to me.

Mark Victor Hansen ~ Through his personal example, Mark taught me that I could Be, Do, and Have whatever my heart desired.

∞ ∞ ∞ ∞ ∞ ∞ ∞

This book is a collaboration between two people from very different backgrounds, and each of us has contributed the expertise gained from our different life paths. John Hanna has provided many financial aspects of this work, and Timothy Marlowe the philosophy and metaphysics. Like a good marriage, the combination of the two has synthesised into a whole that is immeasurably greater than the sum of the parts alone.

Thank you

Timothy Marlowe and John Hanna

Starfishing

There was once a great storm that blew for many days, bringing destruction to the land and whipping the ocean into a seething cauldron of foam and giant waves that scoured the seabed and pounded the shores, day and night. When at last the storm had passed, a young couple went down to the sea at daybreak to look upon the devastation that the tempest had wrought. Standing on a headland they could see by the light of the morning sun, amidst all the driftwood and debris, thousands upon thousands of small dark objects scattered all along the beach. They were too far away to tell what these things might be, but in the distance a small dark figure also appeared, which gradually revealed itself as a man coming up the beach.

He seemed to walk purposefully, but every now and then he would stoop down, then straighten up and toss something into the sea. He did this over and over again, hardly breaking stride, and as he came near the young couple went down to meet him and perhaps learn the reason for his curious behaviour. As they reached the shoreline they realised that the small dark objects were starfish, tens of thousands of starfish washed up on the beach by the ferocity of the storm, and what the man was doing was picking them up one by one and putting them back into the sea.

As the stranger came alongside the young man raised his hand and said, "Excuse me, but we've been watching you for some time. May we ask exactly what it is you're doing with all those starfish?"

The man had been so focused on his task that he looked up a little startled at not being alone, then replied, "Ah, yes. What am I doing here? Well, you see, the storm has washed all these starfish up on the beach, and unless they get back into the water they'll die. I'm just giving them a hand, if you like."

The young woman looked up and down the beach at the countless starfish scattered on the sands, as far as the eye could see, and asked tentatively, "But there are so many, maybe *millions* of them, and you're just one man. What difference can you possibly make to so many starfish?"

The man just smiled gently, bent down, and picking up another starfish threw it even further back into the sea. As he moved on he said, "Made a difference to *that* one, didn't I?"

We're not here to rescue the world, to throw everyone back into the fiscal ocean and save them from the financial storms that sweep through their lives. However, at challenging times along our own journey we have been given a helping hand by many wise, caring men and women, and such gifts come with a responsibility – to share them with others. We may never meet you in person, but if we can make a difference in your life and your future, if we can enrich you with gold or wisdom, then we will have in some small part repaid the gifts we were given. There is nothing more satisfying to the human spirit than making a meaningful contribution to the life of another – so that in giving to you, we also receive again.

And the same principle can apply to you. When you finish this book, if you feel you have been touched, or aided, or inspired, please tell your friends about it. You would be helping us to spread the word, them to change their lives, and yourself to reap the benefits of repaying any gifts you received. Be a starfisher yourself, there's nothing like it.

We're all stars, sometimes we just need a little help to shine.

> *'We are all lying in the gutter,*
> *but some of us are looking at the stars.'*
> ~ Oscar Wilde ~

PART ONE
INNER WEALTH
~ BEING ~

Chapter 1

The Power
It is Within You

'You are what your deep, driving desire is.
As your desire is, so is your will.
As your will is, so is your deed.
As your deed is, so is your destiny.'
~ The Upanishads ~

Have you ever wondered why some people seem to have so much, and others so little? What makes them so different? Is it due to hard work, brains, luck, greed, inheritance? Certainly they all play a part, but they're not crucial, because often those who work the hardest end up with the least, all the intelligent aren't wealthy nor are all the wealthy intelligent, luck always runs out, there are plenty of greedy poor, and most inheritances are squandered. Believe it or not, the most important single factor in the creation of wealth is simply this – *A very strong desire to possess it.* This is the 'being' part of wealth creation. You may think you have that desire, but if you did you'd be wealthy right now. At the end of the chapter we'll tell you why this is so, and that understanding will be a major step on your journey toward achieving lasting wealth and self worth.

The truth is that great wealth is born from great desire, and like all births, it's also challenging. We'd like to begin by telling you a story

1

about how one of us was gifted with that great desire, and though the details may differ, listen for the echoes in your own life as you read. The telling may start out a little grimly, but as with every cloud the silver lining goes all the way 'round.

John's Story ~ Part One

We'd love to introduce you to the extremely powerful ideas and principles that have had such a tremendous impact on our lives, and the lives of those we've been able to share them with. We believe you'll be a richer and wiser person simply by knowing and applying these truths.

My road to financial success had a most inauspicious beginning. Born to a poor family in Egypt where we had enough to live, but no more, we emigrated to Australia in July of 1969. I was seven years old, my brother Paul was just five, and my parents were very excited to be taking us to a new land of opportunity, a 'lucky country' where anyone could start with little or nothing and make a wonderful life for themselves and their family.

But when we arrived, we found the exact opposite of what we hoped for; we were far from fortunate, in fact we weren't lucky at all, and my strongest childhood memory is of my parents worrying and arguing about money long into the night. No matter how hard my father worked as a labourer, which was the only job he could find back then, there was never enough to pay all our bills let alone have what so many other kids took for granted. We never even imagined luxury, we just wanted to have enough to be comfortable and not afraid, but it never happened.

Our first 'home' was one double bed and a kitchen, and all four of us shared the bed. We were lucky there were no mice or cockroaches in the place, thanks to the rats that ate them all. Most days when we came home from school, my little brother and I could look forward to one or two dead rats lying on our floor, but they always multiplied faster than my parents could kill them, just like the bills.

The next place we lived in was a move up in the world, at least vertically – the 16th floor of a housing commission complex overlooking Redfern Oval. The rat numbers dropped, and our diet improved because *my resourceful mother would scatter bread crumbs on our balcony to attract the birds. If she was quick enough we'd have KFP for dinner – Kentucky Fried Pigeon. I also remember going to Pizza Hut for the 'All you can eat for $4.95' offer, stuffing ourselves 'til we thought we'd burst, and then being embarrassed to be sent back for more. My mother would put it in her handbag so we'd have pizza for lunch and dinner the next day, and lunch the day after.*

*One day my father gave me a dollar bill and told me to hop out of the car and get him a pack of cigarettes (in those days kids could do such things), and when I handed them to him he asked for his change from the 98¢. I said it was only 2¢ so I didn't bother, and in his broken English he demanded, "Do you know how **hard** I have to work for 2¢?" So I had to get out of the car and go back into the shop, with my tail between my legs, to ask the shopkeeper for our 2¢. I felt utterly humiliated, and at that moment I swore to myself that I would never grow up like my parents, always struggling for money and never getting ahead or having beautiful things – I made a solemn vow from my heart to be wealthy, and I never forgot. Although I didn't know it at the time, those experiences were gifts, and that was a turning point in my life.*

Poverty and hunger and rats and humiliation are *gifts*? How is that possible? Are we crazy like foxes, or just plain crazy? Wait and see. In the foreword we said that in order to bring about lasting change we'd be addressing not just the outer *doing* but also the inner *being*. The practical world of wealth creation has financial laws that have been developed over centuries, and we'll be covering them. But your inner world of consciousness is ruled by what are called *Universal Principles*, and that's where the real power lies.

A Universal Principle is one that applies everywhere, from the subatomic world to the galactic, from the microscopic to the macroscopic and anywhere in between. If something is true in all those realms then it has tremendous power for growth and transformation, because the universe itself is using it everywhere. Anything else is just a local belief, with much less creative power. So here is the first principle that we'll be sharing with you:

Universal Principle ~1 ~
Voids create Values

Say what? This is the great 'Universal Law' that's going to make such a huge difference in your life? Yes, it is, because those three little words explain everything that human beings do, and why. A void is a sense of need or emptiness, and a value is something that fills that gap. Nature abhors a vacuum and fills it with matter, humans abhor voids and fill them with values. Values are simply the things you care about and that have meaning for you – they motivate you to get up in the morning no matter how life is treating you. Everyone has a set of values; what's most important to them, and second most important, and third, and so on down the list. Whatever is highest in your values is most important to you, and you naturally care about, focus on, and give energy to it.

For example, when you're hungry you think about food, respond to the sight or smell of it, and start to plan what you'd like to eat. When you've just had dinner you'll say, "No thanks," if someone offers you more, because food has temporarily lost its value to you. But the people in the world who are genuinely starving forget about everything else; their entire being is focused on food, and they'll do *anything* to get it. If you've ever experienced real hunger, you know how true this is – the greater the void, the greater the value.

And everyone is run by their values. When something agrees with or supports our values we're drawn towards it and act, but when something challenges our values we're repelled and shut down. Here's how it works in life: We were out driving one day, stopped at an intersection, and a red light windscreen-cleaner sprang from concealment. Shirtless, shaved bald, tattooed, the man stalked between the cars, aggressively brandishing his squeegee. Some just shook their heads, others actually rolled up their windows, but *nobody* wanted him near them. Five minutes later we pulled up at another light and saw the same scenario with a very different outcome. This time a young woman came drifting down between the cars waving a pink squeegee and wearing a tiny pair of beautiful fairy wings. She was such a delight that the first two cars paid for a quick cleaning, while the other drivers smiled at the very sight of her. That's how simple it is – one challenged people's values and made nothing, one supported them and was a success.

So we are motivated to act by our values, and the higher the value the more motivated we are. But here's the secret – *all values are driven by voids*. As we said, a void is an emptiness, something missing, and whatever we feel is most missing in our lives becomes most valuable to us – our top value. If you're thirsty you'll seek water, if you're lonely you'll seek company, if you're tired you'll seek rest, if you're ill you'll seek healing, if you're oppressed you'll seek freedom, if you're dying you'll seek life, and *everything* else becomes secondary. If you're very poor, you'll seek...? Right, your top value can become wealth.

Not only do individuals have voids and values, so do whole societies. In the 1800s, when poverty was widespread and so many children died of disease and hunger, an English advertisement for a food supplement showed a pig's head on a child's body wearing a sailor suit, and the caption read 'Makes Children As Fat As Pigs!' It sounds ridiculous today, but if your children were starving, fatness would be a guarantee of survival. Now that we have so much and we're dying of diseases from too *much* food, voids and values have reversed and thinness is the goal.

So whether you've been aware of it or not, values are the motivators you live your life by. In a very real sense, values dictate your destiny. Whatever you have enough of you tend to take for granted, such as youth or beauty or health or wealth, and you'll only really value them when they're gone. The saying, 'Youth is wasted on the young' is also true as 'Food is wasted on the well-fed' or 'Wealth is wasted on the rich', because real appreciation comes from scarcity.

This takes us back to our question – how were poverty and humiliation a gift to John? By giving him such a tremendous void around wealth that it became his highest value, and set the direction of his life. At the very moment of his greatest humiliation, he felt an overwhelming desire for wealth and his entire consciousness focused on it, guaranteeing that he'd make it happen. From that moment he became a wealth-seeking missile, dedicated to mastering wealth creation. There is no appetite without hunger, and he was *starving*.

Only those who've been hungry really appreciate food, and only the captive know the value of freedom. Because his childhood experiences were so intense, to this day John appreciates wealth and success, is grateful for little things that most take for granted, and has an intense drive to share his hard-earned knowledge with others – deep inside he still wants to help that little boy, and the father and mother that he loved.

'I want to thank my parents for the wonderful gift of poverty.'
~ Roberto Benigni ~
(1999 Oscar acceptance speech as director of the film 'Life Is Beautiful')

So underneath all the theories and philosophy, it's really just that simple; if something is a high value to you, you'll act, and if it's not, you won't. And believe it or not, the great family fortunes of the world – the Rothschilds, Astors, Kennedys, Rockefellers, Hearsts, Gettys – were all built on a foundation of poverty that gave some ancestor the drive to rise up and create a vast fortune. *Voids create values*; this principle underlies all of human history and achievement, and once you start looking you'll find it everywhere.

Here are just a few:

Ian Thorpe was an asthmatic young boy with an allergy to chlorine. He took up swimming to improve his poor health (void) and became one of the greatest swimmers in history.

Donald Trump owed $3.7 billion in the mid-90s (*major* void), refused to declare bankruptcy, and used the spur of that immense debt to drive the recovery to his present $7 billion-plus fortune.

Demosthenes was a junior Athenian politician who was laughed out of the Senate every time he stood up to speak because he had not just an extreme stammer, but also a lisp (void X 2). He was ashamed, and so determined to master speaking that he would go to the shore of the Mediterranean every day, fill his mouth with pebbles so that he had to articulate and focus on every word, and declaim alone to the waves. He not only overcame his handicaps, he became the most powerful speaker of his age, and over 2000 years later he is still known as 'the great orator'.

Charles Atlas was a skinny teenager who couldn't play sports or get a girlfriend, and one day at the beach he was humiliated by a much bigger boy who kicked sand in his face. He was so embarrassed that he went home and began lifting weights – a *lot* of weights. The first exponent of bodybuilding, famous around the world for his extraordinary physique and synonymous with 'muscles', he built a multi-million dollar empire around ads where a 97-pound weakling had sand kicked in his face, trained with Charles, and returned to defeat the bully and win the girl.

Albert Einstein didn't speak until he was four years old, was considered slow and backward in school, and failed mathematics several times. When his father Hermann asked his son's headmaster for advice about the boy's future career, he was told it didn't matter because; "Albert will never amount to anything."

Helen Keller became deaf, mute, and blind at the age of 19 months. Totally cut off from the rest of humanity, she was the first ever deaf and blind person to earn a Bachelor of Arts degree, became a famous speaker and author, met every U.S. president from Grover Cleveland to Lyndon Johnson, and Mark Twain and Charlie Chaplin were among her countless friends. She opened the doors of communication and education for millions.

Mohandas K. Ghandi (the Mahatma, or 'great soul') was a tiny, frail, poor lawyer from a despised and powerless social group in South Africa. Through non-violence and humility, he changed that government's racial discrimination policy, returned to his homeland to almost single-handedly attain India's liberation from the rule of Great Britain, the greatest super-power on earth at the time, and became the champion of oppressed people throughout the world.

Throughout her childhood, all **Wilma Rudolph** wanted to be was a normal little girl. As a toddler, double pneumonia and scarlet fever kept her bedridden while other children played outside. When she was just four years old she contracted polio, which crippled her left leg, forcing her to wear a heavy metal brace. For seven years she and her mother made weekly, 100-mile treks for treatment on her leg, and her brothers and sisters took turns massaging it daily.

When she was 11 years old Wilma finally walked without a brace, and her hope of being normal was in sight. But a strange thing happened. Rather than just keeping up with the other children, she *out-ran* them all. At 16, she won a bronze medal at the 1956 Olympics in Melbourne, and at 20 Wilma Rudolph became the first American woman to win three gold medals – at the 1960 Games in Rome. Fortunately, her dream of becoming a 'normal' child would never come true.

> *'Experience is not what happens to you,*
> *it's what you do with what happens to you.'*
> ~ Aldous Huxley ~

There are countless stories of people whose huge voids became life-giving values: doctors who nearly died as children or lost a loved one to disease, and became healers; millionaires who rose from terrible poverty; the powerless who changed the course of nations. All were faced with challenges that make ours seem insignificant by comparison, and all of them lived the law – Voids Create Values. It's almost enough to make you wish you'd had less pats on the back and more kicks in the butt from life!

And there are just as many stories where children of the wealthy were spared hardship and contracted 'affluenza', a mock malady in which they become unmotivated, ungrateful, self-destructive, and confuse 'want' with 'need'. Their values distorted, with no void around it so taking wealth for granted, they dissipated their fortunes and lives. So if you had a childhood like John's, or you're financially challenged now, don't resent it – it's the seed of your future success. And if you had a comfortable childhood, or are well off now, don't feel bad – there's hope for you, too.

> *'Leave your children enough that they can do anything,*
> *but not so much that they do nothing.'*
> ~ Warren Buffet ~

We'll end this chapter with a profound exercise to awaken the value of wealth in you, but first we'll set the stage so you understand how powerful it is. We promised to explain why, if you really desired wealth, you'd already have it. The answer lies in another principle:

Universal Principle ~ 2 ~
Life Demonstrates Values

It's human nature to give our time, energy, and focus to the things we care about – our values – and whenever we do that success is inevitable. Everyone is always successful in terms of their highest values, so you may *think* you have a high value on wealth, but if you're not rich, you don't. There's a difference between our *true* values and the false or imaginary values we think we *should* have. If you want to know your true values, simply look at your life.

The areas where you're already successful are your true values. If you don't have the wealth you want, it's because you've wanted other things *more*; they were more important to you, and you invested your life force there. This is why not all the poor are motivated to become wealthy. You may have given your time and energy to your family, to some work or cause that inspires you, to owning beautiful things or gaining knowledge; you may have valued your home and garden more than wealth, your animals, wine and food, physical fitness, travel, being a 'good person', or simply freedom and avoiding responsibility.

Whatever it's been for you, that's where your values are, that's where you're already a success, and *that* is the present form of your wealth. All we're going to do now is change your wealth into dollars by linking your present values to finances. Have you noticed how effortless it is to do the things you love, and how hard it is to do the things you don't? Again, that's the power of values. You are not and never have been a failure, you've always been highly successful in terms of your true values, and now you're going to be successful in wealth. In fact, if you truly value it you can't *not* succeed – it's the law.

'You give birth to that on which you fix your mind.'
~ Antoine de Saint-Exupery ~

And just to make sure that every level of your mind is aligned with wealth, we'd like to address one more fundamental issue. At first you may think this doesn't apply to you, but it permeates the world and is very difficult to avoid picking up unconsciously. We've all heard the sayings many times: from the West we're told, 'The meek shall inherit the earth,' 'It is better to give than to receive,' and 'The love of money is the root of all evil,' while from the East we hear, 'It is easier for a camel to pass through the eye of a needle than for a rich man to enter the kingdom of heaven.'

You know them by heart, but have you considered their implications? The strange thing about these odd ideas is that if you really lived them you'd have and be virtually nothing, yet the institutions that teach them are among the wealthiest and most powerful on earth. They're neither meek nor poor, and if they had been they would not have survived to attract vast wealth from believers of their myths.

The truth is that there's nothing inherently bad or evil about wealth, just as poverty doesn't necessarily create kindness or goodness. Take a moment to really think about the people you've met in your life. If you're honest, you'll see that the wealthy can be just as generous and kind as the poor, and the hard-hearted poor are perfectly balanced by wealthy ones. Extreme poverty can be as distorting and corrupting as extreme wealth; in fact, the qualities are not in the money, but in *us*. Rich or poor, all have human nature and are who they are.

Desiring wealth does not make you a bad person; nobody with more than you will ever call you greedy. In fact, they're more likely to see you as a loser because you settled for so little. Only those with less than you have would even think it, as they'll be thought greedy by those with less than *they* have – it's all a matter of perspective.

So just in case you're carrying even a microscopic trace of the belief that wealth is somehow impure, or that you'll be magically rewarded in heaven for having nothing here on earth, this may be your time to let it go. Don't sabotage your potential for a myth, don't teach your children to settle for less than they're worth, don't trade your inner truth for a clever outer lie. Every time you say, "I don't care about money, it means nothing to me, there are more important things in life," you're literally throwing away thousands and possibly *millions* of dollars, because what we think and believe determines the course of our lives.

If you're kind and caring now you'll be the same with great wealth, and if you're petty or vindictive, having money by itself won't change that. So given that whether you're rich or poor you're still going to be *you*, why not choose rich? What have you got to lose, except your poverty and illusions?

*'Money can't change people,
it just helps them become who they really are.'*
~ Grandpa Simpson ~

~ Exercise ~

All you need to transform your life right now is a pen and paper, and the more honest you are the more powerful this will be. Set aside two hours to look at the values your life *demonstrates* – not what you imagine they are, but what you give your time and energy and thought and money to, the things you make sure are a part of your day no matter what. These are your true values, so you're going to list them in order of their demonstrated priority to you. We can fool ourselves about what our values really are, but we can't fool our life.

Let's say yours are family, health, and travel, in that order. Take your top value, and begin writing down, one benefit per line, how having vast wealth will help your family: a bigger home, better food, quality education for the kids, tutors, the best medical care, a swimming pool, travel, beautiful possessions (list them all), horses, a holiday home, etc. Look at the 7 areas of life; spiritual, mental, career, financial, family, social, and physical. Look at the past and how money *could* have helped, at the future and how it *can* help, at the present and how it *will* help.

And don't just write a list, *feel* what it would be like to have and be able to give these things to the people you love. Be creative, imaginative, focused, lateral… dig deep, because this is important. If you don't finish in one session, continue later and keep adding insights. Whatever your top value is, don't stop until you have listed 200 benefits wealth will provide to that area of your life. The more you link them, the more motivated you'll be.

We've taken enough people through this exercise to know the value of that number, so don't waste time thinking you can't do it – you can, if you don't give up. Stop at 50 and you'll notice some effect in your mind, but it won't last. At 100, your focus will begin to shift. At 150 you'll become aware that you actually feel different, and if you're disciplined enough to link 200 benefits of wealth to your highest value, the outer world will respond and things will change for you in the most extraordinary way. From out of the blue ideas will come to you, opportunities will arise, people will appear – things will start to *happen!*

You already had the ability to fulfil your values as they were; linking wealth piggy-backs on that power, and starts to manifest it in exactly the same way. And the best part of it is that you needn't sacrifice the things you love, you just *use* them to create your new life. If you're serious, you'll do the same thing with your second highest value, and then your third. Find 200 ways wealth will benefit your health, and your exploration of the world, or whatever your values are. When you do, you'll be motivated and magnetic to a degree you've never experienced before, because what you think about you bring about.

Muscles only grow when you exercise them, and it's the same with all your faculties. The content of each chapter is the *inspiration* (we work), the exercises are the *perspiration* (you work), and together they can create a *revelation* (the universe works). All it takes is a little discipline for your future to align with your dreams. Once it happens for you, you won't doubt the power of values.

If you're surprised to find no financial information in the first chapter of a book on money, there is a reason. We're laying the foundation for lasting wealth and, like a garden, the better you prepare the soil the faster and deeper grow the roots. Your mind is the soil your wealth will grow from, so we dig deeply. We intend to take you to places you've never been before, both inside and out, and in the next chapter we'll take another step toward transforming your financial frog into a prince or princess.

'It is funny about life.
If you refuse to accept anything but the very best,
you will very often get it.'
~ W. Somerset Maugham ~

Chapter 2

The Decision
The Buck Stops Here

'It is fatal to enter into any struggle
without the desire to win it.'
~ Napoleon Bonaparte ~

Let's begin this chapter with a wake-up call, and then a myth-breaker. Did you know that 90-95% of lottery winners are broke again in five years, and that 50% of them are actually poorer than they were before? How is this even possible, let alone almost inevitable? It's not that they were particularly foolish, because almost everyone does it. The answer lies in one word – *Responsibility*. People buy lottery tickets because they don't believe they can make it themselves, and hope that luck will save them. That's unwise, and almost all of the tiny percentage who win become even less responsible, throwing the money away like drunken sailors. The result is that wealth almost destroys them, what should have been a blessing becomes a curse, and they carry the regret for the rest of their lives. For most of us, losing even a thousand dollars is emotionally stressful – imagine how you'd feel if you lost *millions*.

The problem is that they failed to understand how their world had changed. They didn't grow their character with their wealth, and stayed poor *inside*. They hadn't learned how to manage money, and didn't feel they deserved it, so even when they managed to attract it temporarily they couldn't hold onto it. Without knowledge and discipline, money alone won't transform your life. Wealth is one of the powers of this world, and with great power comes great responsibility. What happens if you don't respect your loved ones and associates? They leave you, and money is just the same, so you want to be as wise as possible *before* it arrives – that's where we come in.

> *'Winning the lottery is like throwing*
> *Miracle-Gro on your character defects.'*
> ~ Friend of lottery winner ~

And don't imagine the problem is that there just isn't enough wealth in the world, or that the cunning and corrupt wealthy have conspired to keep everyone else poor. As we said in Chapter 1, the power lies within you; there are no victims in this world, and believe it or not, you are the master of your own fate. This little story illustrates why.

In the early 90s the American TV show 'Lifestyles of the Rich and Famous' was hosted by Robyn Leach, and for the first and only time the Vatican allowed filming in the chambers and catacombs beneath the city. Their guide opened doors that had been closed to outsiders for centuries, and the film crew was overwhelmed by the fabulous gold, silver, jewels, ancient statues, Old Master paintings, and priceless manuscripts. Afterwards, a dazzled Robyn said on air that at a conservative estimate, there was enough wealth stored beneath the Vatican to make every single man, woman, and child on earth a millionaire several times over.

Amazing enough, but here's the incredible part. If it was actually shared out, so that we all became millionaires overnight, it would make no difference to the distribution of wealth on the planet. Within a very short time, and with very few exceptions, that vast river of wealth would flow out and redistribute itself in exactly the same way. Those who are wealthy now would simply have more wealth, and today's poor would be poor again – because it's not about what you *have*, it's all about who you *are*.

It's not society, or greed, or unfairness that allocates wealth, it's our own *consciousness*, and it will avoid us until we learn to honour it, just like any other part of life. Gold bars are like Olympic gold medals – they go to those who master the skills. Like water, if you don't prepare a way for wealth in your mind and heart, how can you expect it to flow to you?

'With your mind you create the world.'
~ The Buddha ~

John's Story ~ Part Two

Although the poverty and the crucial 2¢ were pivotal experiences in my life, I didn't know it at the time, and many more years of struggle were to pass until I realised that I already had everything I needed to become the person I longed to be. My father wanted my brother and me to have a better life than he did, and for him the key to that better life was something he never had – an education. So even though I'd just cruised through school, I was sent off to university to study accounting and make something of myself. I didn't want to disappoint him, and didn't know what else to do anyway, but I found accounting mind-numbingly boring. After four tedious years I decided that all I really wanted to do was make money, so to my father's horror I dropped out.

*Once out in the real world I found, to my own horror, that university hadn't taught me even how to make money, let alone become wealthy. What it **had** prepared me for was to work for the wealthy and powerful, and that was not my dream. I knew my father was right about education being the key, but we differed on what kind of education that should be. I realised that if wealth was in my future, no one was going to hand it to me – it was up to me to make it happen, so I began to educate myself.*

Now that it was about my values, my attitude to study changed completely; I devoured every book on wealth I could find, and attended the seminars of every financial teacher, mentor, or guru who came to town. One man who had a huge impact on my life was Robert Kiyosaki, a self-made millionaire and the author of 'Rich Dad, Poor Dad'. I sat with 200 people listening to him speak, but to me there was no one in the room but the two of us, and every word he said was like gold.

He said, "If you want to become successful, whatever that means to *you, learn to stay above the line." Then he drew a horizontal line on the whiteboard and said, "Above this line are the successful, and below it is everybody else. The word on this line that defines and separates them is... Responsibility. Successful people take responsibility for everything that happens to them, and that means exactly what it says – **everything**. The bottom of the pile is made up of people who avoid taking responsibility for their lives, and as a result they are victims, puppets, corks on the sea of life."*

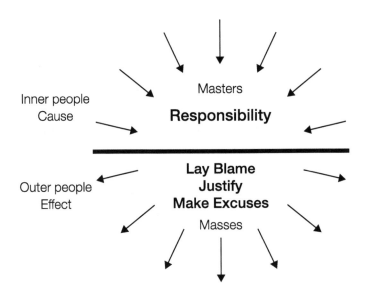

That was a revelation to me, and over the years my appreciation for the power of his words has continued to grow. As I applied the principle of responsibility, my life gradually began to change. Because I was young and impatient, I set myself the goal of becoming a millionaire in one year. As it turned out, it took five.

'Take your life in your own hands, and what happens?
A terrible thing – no one to blame.'
~ Erica Jong ~

We've found 7 major differences between the wealthy and successful, and those who are not. They are the 7 financial laws in this book, and by following them to the letter you'll soon find yourself switching sides. But the wealthy start by doing *one* thing right, the first and most important of the differences – they accept full responsibility for their own lives, and don't expect anyone else to lead or support or rescue them. In contrast, the others do *three* things which explain why they are where they are. So what are the three powerful habits that make people so powerless in their lives?

1. They Make Excuses.
2. They Justify Themselves.
3. They Lay Blame.

Those living below the line constantly make excuses for why they have or haven't done something, are full of justifications for why their life is the way it is, and continually blame forces outside themselves for their circumstances. "It's my lazy partner, my boss, interest rates, the kids, the economy, the government, the weather. I'm too young, I'm too old, too happy, too sad, too tired, too busy, too…" always an excuse, and never a reason.

Life is about cause and effect, and those above the line are the cause of their own lives – they know the power is inside and *act* to have what they want. The below-the-liners believe the power is outside themselves, so they are always at *effect*, and they get what's left. That is the basis for our first financial law:

Financial Law ~ 1 ~
If It's To Be, It's Up To Me

Of course we all face challenges that test us, and no one stays above the line 100% of the time, but there is a direct correlation between how much responsibility you accept and your success in every area of life. Those who live above the line are what we call 'inner people', while below the line are 'outer people'. Inner people meet challenges not by complaining or blaming, but by asking themselves motivating questions like, *How can I earn more money? How can I reduce my debt? How can I improve my circumstances? What can I do to get more out of my life?* Their focus is on 'What can *I* do?' The quality of your life is determined by the quality of the questions you ask, and inner people ask themselves high quality questions, so they rise to high quality positions in life.

During World War II, U.S. President Harry S Truman kept a small wooden plaque on his desk that said, *The Buck Stops Here*, to remind himself and everyone else that he was responsible – for *everything*. Ultimately directing the outcome of the war, his decisions influenced the world's future. Rudy Guiliani is widely recognised as one of New York City's greatest mayors; on his desk he also had a plaque, and his said simply, *I'm Responsible*. Because these men were willing to accept great responsibility, they were given tremendous power.

Zenzi – 'You have no one to blame but yourself.'
Traditional African name, to give courage in life's difficulties.

On the other hand, outer people focus on the problem rather than the solution, and continually complain to themselves and anyone who will listen about how hard life is. Instead of taking action they wait for circumstances to change, or their mood to lift, or for something or someone to rescue them, and that not only doesn't work, it wastes precious time. As long as they make the problem outside themselves, the solution will be too, and they become powerless victims of circumstance. If an outer person gets a flat tyre, they curse the road and the car and the other drivers, they moan about why things like this always happen to them, and argue about whose turn it is to fix it. An inner person gets out, changes the tyre, and drives on.

Which behaviour describes you? Are you above the line or below it? Your answer will describe where you are right now, and if you're honest you'll probably be more below than above. That's the bad news, but the good news is that by changing your behaviour you can change your life.

'The greatest discovery of my generation is that people can transform their lives by altering their perceptions and attitudes of thought.'
~ William James ~ 'The Father of Modern Psychology'

John ~ Continued

Robert Kiyosaki helped me become an inner person, and put me on track to the wealth I swore to have as a child. However, education is never done, it's a life-long commitment to keep growing. In July of 2000, a friend recommended that I attend another seminar given by a man named Dr John F. Demartini. Something inside, that little voice that seems to know more than we do, told me to go, and my life hasn't been the same since. Founder of the 'Demartini Institute', and the author of dozens of books, Dr Demartini travels the world speaking on inspiration, purpose, and wealth creation. One of the first things he said to me turned my world upside-down, and it's the third Universal principle we want to share with you.

Universal Principle ~ 3 ~
The One and the Many

Put simply, this law states that everything is arranged in a hierarchy, with many at the bottom and progressively fewer as you rise to the top. The clearest image for this concept is the pyramid, with its broad base and narrow apex, and it applies to all areas and levels of existence.

For example, physically: everyone exercises, even if only to walk to the kitchen or lift the TV remote; there are fewer (but still many) who exercise as a daily discipline; still fewer athletes go on to compete at the local, state, national, or international levels; fewer Olympians; even fewer gold medallists; and at the top of each field only one Michael Jordan, Tiger Woods, or Usain Bolt.

In education: most people go to primary school; fewer go on to high school and university; fewer still earn bachelor or master's degrees, or doctorates; even fewer become emeritus professors; and there is only one annual Nobel Prize winner in each field, one Albert Einstein, one Stephen Hawking.

Again, in wealth: 60% of the world lives in poverty; fewer live above subsistence; fewer still are wealthy; even fewer are millionaires; billionaires are even rarer; and there's only one Bill Gates or King Feisal or Rothschild in each area of the globe.

And to show that the principle is truly universal: there are countless subatomic particles, fewer atoms and molecules, fewer individual beings, fewer continents, fewer still planets, increasingly fewer stars, galaxies, galaxy clusters, super-galaxies, super-galaxy clusters, and only one universe.

In every case, there is the *One* (the Master) at the top and the *Many* (the Masses) at the bottom. Wherever you look, it just seems to be the way the universe is set up. It's a fact, but an unwelcome and seemingly unfair one if you cling to the myth that everyone can be wealthy if they just work hard enough, study long enough, or are given enough help. Americans like to say, 'Anybody can become President,' but that's deceptive – anybody *can*, but very few ever *will*, and it's exactly the same with wealth. The only ones who achieve wealth are those with the determination to do so, and the will to do what everyone else avoids. 'If it's to be, it's up to me,' and nothing else can get you there.

> *'Family, religion, friendship;*
> *these are the three demons you must slay*
> *if you wish to succeed in business.'*
> ~ Mr Burns ~

You needn't go quite so far as this wonderfully deranged billionaire, but rising up the wealth ladder definitely takes something special, because statistically the odds are against you.

World Wealth Distribution
70 million, only 1%, have extreme wealth.
1.2 billion have varying degrees of relative wealth.
4.3 billion live from poverty to subsistence.
1.5 billion live in abject poverty, on $200-$1000 per annum.

The Law of the One and the Many cannot be avoided, and it's up to you to decide which you're going to be – a master, or one of the masses. If you choose mastery, then you must accept responsibility for your life like never before; thoughts, words, actions, results, rewards. Only by becoming your own cause can you determine the effects you have on the world. And if you're still clinging to the hope that everyone can stand on the top of a pyramid at once, because it's such a tempting fantasy, try to think of any place or time that has ever been true. Realise that it's not, and never has been, possible.

> *'Be grateful for the losers; without them,*
> *the rest of us could not succeed.'*
> ~ Anon ~

We'd love to think we can all be equally wealthy and successful, but it doesn't happen in nature, and it doesn't happen in our world either – it's a hierarchy, and it's competitive, and only the best succeed. There's a great old joke that illustrates this principle very well. Two men were walking along a jungle path when suddenly a tiger appeared in front of them and began to creep forward, snarling. They both turned and fled for their lives, and as they ran they could hear the tiger gaining on them in great leaps.

One man turned to the other and said in despair, "This is hopeless, nobody can outrun a tiger."

The other man, a clear-sighted pragmatist, just put his head down and said, "I don't have to outrun the tiger. I just have to outrun *you*."

It's funny, wise, and true.

Please understand this: knowledge, wisdom, power, money, are never in the hands of the masses, they have always been in the hands of the masters, and the only choice you have is where you want to play in the game. Once you genuinely decide to take responsibility for your own life, everything else falls into place. Leaving the herd may be a little scary, but at least you won't get trampled like these unfortunate followers:

In the late 1920s, America was gripped by stock market mania; almost everyone was investing all they had and borrowing more, looking to get rich quick. Early in 1929, the millionaire Bernard Baruch got a hot stock tip from a shoeshine boy. He went to his office, called his broker, and said, *"Sell me out! When shoeshine boys are giving tips it's time to get out of the market."*

Six months later came Black Friday and the worst stock market crash in history, triggering The Great Depression. Baruch was so masterful that a little incident which most would have ignored prompted him to take immediate action, so he survived when millions were ruined and the world plunged into a decade of hardship. Because he understood mass consciousness, not only did Baruch save his fortune, he re-invested at the bottom of the market and increased it.

Now, we know the magnitude of what we're asking you to do. This is a life-altering decision, and once you genuinely make it the repercussions will affect your entire life. It's easy to take responsibility and credit when things are going well, when the sun is shining and there's money in your pocket, but it takes real strength of character to do it in times of darkness and uncertainty. Giving up complaint and blame is a powerful change to make, but there are no mistakes or randomness in the universe, so if you're reading this book then you may be ready to take that step.

Acknowledge that it's your nature to rise. Nobody wakes up in the morning and says, "I want to be less! I want less intelligence, less love, less wealth in my life!" You are here to grow and to shine, as is everyone in their own time. The question is, is this your time? All you need do is *decide*, and then *act*. All that's been holding you back is self-doubt, which comes from a lack of knowledge and experience, and you're gaining that now.

'You can have whatever you want.'
'No, only some people get what they want.'
'That's true – they're the ones who show up to get it.'
~ Antonio Banderas ~ in 'Take The Lead'

~ EXERCISE ~

This chapter began with a wake-up, and it's ending the same way. In order to get where you want to go it's vital to know where you are now, and there is a direct correlation between a person's wealth and their knowledge of it. In other words, the richer people are, the more exactly they know what they have and how much they're worth. And of course, the opposite is true; poor people haven't a clue, and don't want to know, about their financial situation. They're like the mythical ostrich burying its head in the sand, and for the same reason – fear. This exercise will help you accept Responsibility with a capital 'R'.

So get out your pen and paper, you're going to wake up and get honest. Draw a line down the centre of the page, head one side 'Assets' and the other 'Liabilities', and just start listing. On the left side of the page write down everything you own and its worth if you were to sell it. That means house, car, motorcycle, property, furniture, savings, shares, investments, clothes, art, books, appliances… everything! If you're not sure, take the average between your estimate and your partner's. If it's just you, then average out your most optimistic and pessimistic estimates.

Then on the right side of the page write down everything you owe and the exact amounts. If you don't know, go look! Find out, do some research, this is well worth the effort. Use this exercise to start getting your financial house in order – there's only one letter difference between the words 'own' and 'owe', but they are worlds apart.

When you've finished go back and check it over, then wait a day or two to recall anything you may have forgotten. Then total both sides, subtract liabilities from assets, and that is your financial position at this moment. If your number is a large positive, congratulations! You've done quite well so far, possibly better than you thought, so you know you can do it and we'll help you do even better.

If your number is small, then the illusion has been shattered. You can admit your true situation and begin to turn things around.

If your number is negative, congratulations! You are in the excellent position of being not only highly motivated, but also humbled enough to accept guidance that can help you change. Remember what Donald

Trump's number was at one time – it makes yours look pretty good, doesn't it?

But whatever your number, it's neither good nor bad, it's just what it is at this moment. Now that you know where you are, you can begin to climb. So don't despair, get motivated! *Use* the number to your advantage. Look at your age and what you have right now, project it into the future, and ask yourself, "Is that a fair exchange for the precious years of my life?" If not, make a firm decision right now, just as John did with his 2¢ lesson, that you'll do whatever it takes to create the wealth you'd love to have.

And even though it can be challenging at first, remember:

'The pain of regret far outweighs the pain of discipline.'

Choose a life of what could be, not what might have been.

Chapter 3

The Plan
Blueprint of Destiny

"Would you tell me, please,
which way I ought to go from here?"
"That depends a good deal
on where you want to get to," said the Cat.
"I don't care much where..." said Alice.
"Then it doesn't matter which way you go."
~ Lewis Carroll, Alice in Wonderland ~

In order to get here, you should have completed two steps by now: one, created a strong determination to become wealthy by linking it to your top values; and two, accepted full responsibility for your life and be willing to take action to change it. If you haven't done both, *go and do them now* – we'll wait. This is no joke; if you're serious about financial mastery, every step is crucial, and each one builds on the last. You don't climb a ladder by missing a rung, and it's the same with the ladder of success. Unlike Alice, you *know* where you want to go, so your direction is important. We know from experience that in five years' time the difference between doing the exercises and merely reading the words will be dramatic, and measurable in dollars. Do the work now, the rewards are worth it.

Now, let's begin this chapter with the next financial law – another secret and crucial quality that distinguishes the successful from everyone else.

Financial Law ~ 2 ~
You Must Have a Written Plan

For some reason, most people resist doing this as fiercely as dogs resist having a bath, but successful people do the things that others won't, and this is one of them. We can't overstate the vital importance of putting down on paper the plan for your financial future. Have you noticed that if you go shopping without a list, you get home and then smack yourself on the forehead because you've forgotten something? And more often than not, it's the one thing you really wanted in the first place – you can always go back to the store, although it's annoying, but you can't get back the lost time. Financial plans are for a lifetime, and time lost here can be years or even decades.

'Fail to plan, plan to fail.'

It's a catchy little line, and very true. Would you go on holiday without planning where you're going, when, the cost, and how you'll pay for it? Ignoring the details is asking for trouble, but most people approach wealth in exactly that way – they put more planning into a weekend away than creating financial security, and then are shocked when they have none. Doesn't your financial future deserve at least as much care as you give to shopping, holidays, moving house, and all the countless little things you wouldn't consider doing without some kind of plan?

That's a rhetorical question and of course the answer is yes, but there's an ancient truth that says, 'To know and not to do is not to know.' In our seminars we ask people to raise their hands if they believe in planning for their future, and virtually every hand in the room goes up, except for the rugged individualists who refuse to listen to anyone. (Coincidentally, they also seem to learn the least.) We then ask them to keep their hand up if they have a written financial plan *right now* that describes what they're going to do, how they're going to do it, and what outcome they expect to achieve, with contingency plans.

Almost all the hands that went up so confidently then come down, sheepishly, because even though we *know* how important it is, we don't do it – therefore, we don't really know. Significantly, the few who keep their hands up are about the same percentage as those who retire with the financial security and freedom to enjoy life after working so hard for 50 years. It comes down to this: if you want something, you must *value* it, and that means doing whatever it takes to make it happen – including making the dreaded plans.

> ### *'Oh, why do the things that happen to stupid people keep happening to ME!?'*
> ~ Homer Simpson ~

Plans not only make your path clearer for you, they're also a request to life and the world. If you don't tell anyone what you want for your birthday, even though you know exactly, what happens? At best you get things you don't really want, and at worst you get nothing at all. Well, the universe is the same, and if you don't tell it what you want, how can it give it to you? You have to *ask* for what you want in every area of life, or prepare to be disappointed. The same principle applies not only metaphysically, but also physically.

If you say to a builder, "Build me a house. Go!" what do you think will happen? That's right, nothing, because the first thing he'll ask is, "Where are the plans?"

But if you say to him, "I want a house here. Two stories high, 250 square metres, with a three metre foundation, three bedrooms and two baths, a study, a living room, a spiral wooden staircase, a big kitchen looking out over the garden, a slate roof, a big swimming pool out back, a curving driveway…" and keep describing it in so much detail that he can literally see it in his mind's eye, it will be built.

Well, you're building yourself a financial house, and the more clearly you can see it, the more surely it will happen. Writing down your goals and dreams is the first step in giving them life, a vital stage in translating vague ideas and hopes into reality. Anything left in your head tends to stay there, but the simple act of bringing it out and writing it down greatly increases the likelihood of it actually happening. Writing is a commitment, hence the expression, *Get it in writing*. There is magic to writing – use it.

'A short pencil is more powerful than a long memory when it comes to bringing dreams into reality.'

We're going to show you how to do it, then we want you to write down exactly how you'd love your financial future, because if you don't decide how it's going to be, somebody else will. Any area of your life you don't empower with your energy and vision, somebody else over-powers, and they won't care about your dream. Writing gives you the chance to see what you actually think, and to become aware of what hasn't even occurred to you. We guarantee that any detail you leave out, anything that you're not prepared for, will become the stumbling block you'll face in trying to make your dream a reality. But anything you plan for flows much more smoothly. The choice is simple – be a planner, or become a statistic.

When you write, make your plan so clear and concise that you can *see* it, and *feel* it. Keep refining every paragraph until you know; "That's it!" If you're still uncertain about any part, keep on refining until you're clear. It then becomes a visual image, and at that point your mind is able to see clearly what you want to create. Honour yourself enough to write down in detail the future that you'd love.

'Where there is no vision, the people perish.'
~ Proverbs 29.18 ~

Have you ever woken up in the middle of the night with an idea and been so inspired that you just had to write it down? It was like a spark you wanted to capture, and you couldn't wait another minute, you wanted to start *now*. That's one of the signs of true inspiration, that you don't hesitate; procrastination is powerless, action is inspired.

When you're inspired and act on something, you'll have energy in direct proportion to your clarity. If you're clear about what you want and can *see* it in your mind, you'll have the vitality to do it. It's only when you don't know or are unclear that you hesitate and lack the energy to achieve something.

'Your vitality is proportionate to the vividness of your vision.'
~ Dr John F. Demartini ~

The truly important and valuable things in life are never easy. Every goal, great or small, attracts both support and challenge – things that assist us, and things that make us grow stronger. When you act you'll be supported *and* challenged, and you need both, but when the going gets tough many people say, "Well, I guess it wasn't meant to be." That's fear talking, because the challenge is just a test of your commitment. When it gets too challenging most people give up, and then wonder why they're not manifesting their goals and dreams in life. That's *our* goal, to help you break through any barriers to creating your dreams.

'It's not strength that matters, it's focus.'
~ Bruce Lee ~

We have a limited capacity to absorb facts and information, but stories flow in easily because they speak to a much older and deeper part of us. One simple tale often communicates more effectively than an ocean of statistics. Here's a pertinent story from Tim's professional life.

Tim ~ Part I

For the past 15 years I've been using universal principles to help people through challenging times, from depression, to fear of public speaking, relationship problems, bankruptcy, loss of purpose, loss of a loved one, and everything in between. Early in my career as a consultant an exhausted-looking man came to my office one day after being referred by another client. When we sat down I asked how I could be of service to him, and he didn't waste a moment on chit-chat.

His first words were, "I know you can't help me, and I only came because my friend who recommended you is very worried about me. The truth is, my life has fallen apart and I don't expect to be here much longer. I've had enough, and there's nothing anybody can do about it."

31

He was clearly near the end of his tether, so I told him I'd had some remarkable experiences in my work and no longer believed anything was impossible. I said, "But since you're here anyway, you've got nothing to lose by telling me what happened, have you? Maybe I can surprise you." What followed was a 90-minute conversation, so I'll condense it to the essential points.

He smiled faintly and said, "Sure, why not? I have... no, I **had** a very successful mortgage finance business until two weeks ago. Two years ago a friend's wife left him, he got fired from his job, and he was living in his car. I felt so sorry for the guy that I asked him to come work for me, even though I knew he wasn't right for the job. A year later I promoted him to manager because he was hopeless at sales, and I felt sorry for him again.

"One morning two weeks ago I came in to work to find the front door chained, all the office equipment and furniture and phones and staff gone, and the bank accounts cleaned out. He'd taken everything to set up his own business – mine – and now I have nothing left. Believe it or not, this is the third time it's happened to me and I just can't take it anymore. I don't want to live in a world where people act like this."

I knew that if he didn't find a way through this crisis, there was a good chance he'd carry out his threat – you learn to feel who's genuine and who's not. But I also know that we each create our own destiny, so the first thing I said was, "So when you first hired this man, what did the little voice inside say?"

He paused a moment, then laughed and said, "I remember it very clearly; it said, 'Don't do it, don't hire him.'"

"But you ignored it."

"Well, yes. He was so depressed and I..."

"You wanted to rescue him."

"Right."

I said, "Well, that's two reasons why you're in this fix right now. First, you ignored your intuition that told you not to hire him. Have you ever parked your car somewhere, had a feeling you shouldn't, and when you came back it was scratched or had a ticket?"

He nodded, and I went on, "I can't tell you how many people I've *seen in some desperate situation because they ignored the voice that told them not to do it. Our intuition is a source of innate knowing and wisdom, and it's just waiting for the chance to help us direct our life. It's so important to listen to it that every time we don't, we get a painful lesson to make sure we pay attention next time. Can you see how much it cost you not to listen?"*

He rubbed his jaw and said, "About $250,000, my business, my health, and maybe my life."

"It knew this was coming and tried to protect you; are you going to listen next time? Have you got the message?"

"Absolutely!"

"Great, then it was worth it. That voice can help you regain everything you lost and more, if you just listen to it. Second, you rescued him – twice! Don't you know that rescuing people is one of the most destructive thing you can do to them? It says, 'You poor bugger, you can't make it on your own so I'll help you,' and even though they may seem grateful at the time, they resent you for it. Has this experience taught you not to rescue people?"

He laughed and said, "Well, if this is the result, yes!"

"Okay, that's two vital things you've learned. Good."

He was looking more interested, not so grey and defeated, so now that he had the energy I shocked him with, "So what part of you wanted this to happen?"

He spluttered; "What? What do you mean?"

I said, "There are no victims in this world, and nothing happens to us randomly, so what part of you wanted to get rid of that business?"

He went completely still, looked me in the eyes for the first time, and said, "You know, I actually hated that company. I knew we were ripping those poor people off and I felt so guilty about it, but I couldn't walk away from the money."

I asked him, "So the richer you got, the worse you felt?"

"Absolutely."

"And what do you think the effect of years of intense guilt and shame would be?"

"I'd probably have a heart attack or cancer, just to escape it."

"Has it ever occurred to you to thank this man for saving your life?"

"No... but it does now."

"And thank him for teaching you not to rescue people and listen to your intuition? That's priceless."

He said slowly, *"I can't believe I'm saying this, but it was a bargain."*

"How do you feel about the loss of your company now?"

"Relieved, actually."

"And what about the other two times this happened?"

"Aha! They were both successful companies that I started, then hated but couldn't leave, and somebody I trusted stole them from me. They all rescued me from myself! I never saw it this way before." He was getting excited now, and not at all tired – the truth does set you free.

"Did they feel guilty about the way those companies made money?"

"Hell, no, they didn't care."

"So what does this tell you about yourself?"

He thought a minute and then said slowly, *"That I have... integrity,"* and his eyes filled with tears.

"Right! Also that you have an exceptional mind for business, and others respect the ideas you've had more than you do, which is why they got the money from them. Those profits were killing you because you felt so guilty about the way you made them, right?"

He nodded dazedly and I went on, *"So instead of just doing what you can get away with, why not plan something you'd love to do? You obviously have the skills, you just haven't applied them wisely. Do you have any ideas for what you'd like to do next?"*

"Heaps! I was just too depressed to even think about starting again, but I've got so many great ideas!"

We spent a short time discussing them, but he kept glancing at his watch and shifting in his chair, so I asked him, *"Do you have an appointment?"* and he said something wonderful; *"Actually, I just can't wait to get out there and start my new business – one that I can really be proud of."*

In 90 minutes he went from despair to inspiration because he understood *why* things had happened the way they did, and had a plan to ensure they didn't happen again. Without a clear plan for his life he ended up doing whatever came along, and because his heart wasn't in it, it kept falling apart on him. If he'd known what he wanted from the start he could have created *that* life, and saved himself years of time, effort, and money. Plans can not only make your life, they can also save it.

So here is a 7-step outline for writing your financial plan. The details and size of the vision will vary with each person, but the basic pattern is the same. And if you follow this procedure, the magnitude of your vision will increase steadily – as you *do* and *have* more, you'll automatically feel you *deserve* more, and the moment you're certain you deserve something, you can have it.

1 ~ What Do I Really Want?

Before you start writing, sit down and do some thinking. What exactly do you want from your life? You may be surprised to realise you've never really taken the time to get clear on this – like most people, too caught up in day-to-day living to plan life itself. If so, this is an excellent time to start. Think about your financial goals and needs; time frames – that is, by *when* do you want something; possessions; homes; savings; investments; royalties; businesses; etc. Keep it affirmative by focusing on the things you want rather than those you don't – 'great health and the best medical care', rather than 'not get cancer and avoid public wards'. You're limited only by your imagination, so consider not just what you think you could get by on, but what you'd love to have.

2 ~ Write Your Goals Down.

We've already discussed how and why the act of writing is so powerful, and now you're going to do it. After clarifying the broad strokes of your financial masterpiece in Step 1, simply write them all down. And remember to not just write lists, but simultaneously *see* and *feel* what it would be like to actually have these things. Start with a rough draft, but when you've written and refined and ordered it all, put it in a beautiful book. This is your dream and your future, so honour it. The more respect you give your plan, and the more time and space you allot it in your mind and life, the sooner it will happen.

3 ~ Be Specific.

'God is in the detail.' The more specific you are, the easier it is to manifest something. The more uncertain you are, the harder it is and the longer it takes. Don't just say, "I want more money." How much, exactly? The universe tends to be quite literal in its responses, so if you want another $100,000, say so. Otherwise, you could end up with $10, because that's 'more money'. Don't just say, "I'd like an investment property." Where will it be, how much will it cost, what's the rent, is it an apartment, house, block of flats, commercial premises, factory? It's important to write down the details; vagueness loses energy, clarity increases it.

> *'One never climbs so high*
> *as when he knows where he is going.'*
> ~ Napoleon Bonaparte ~

4 ~ Be Realistic.

That means don't aim too high or too low, neither wildly optimistic nor grimly pessimistic, but write down what is actually possible for you at this time. If you write something that's too small and easy, you won't be inspired about it. But if it's too big you'll be intimidated, won't believe in it, and you'll lose heart. It's important to keep your promises, especially to yourself, and if the plan is too big you'll train yourself not to do what you say. There are no unrealistic goals, just unrealistic time frames. Like Goldilocks, you have to find what's not too soft or too hard, but j-u-u-ust right. Don't worry, if you continue with these strategies you'll be regularly updating and upgrading your vision, but you must start somewhere.

> *'A good plan today is better than a perfect plan tomorrow.'*

5 ~ Make Your Goals Measurable.

In order to stay on track, it's vital to know where you are. Otherwise, how would you know when you've achieved a goal and it's time to extend it, or create a new one? It's also important to keep yourself motivated by celebrating your successes. 'Financial independence' is vague and unmeasurable, and will change as you grow. If you want $1,000,000 in 10 years, that's $100,000 a year, $1,923 a week, $274 a day, or an extra $34 an hour per eight-hour day. Not only will you know exactly where you are and what to do next, but $34 an hour is a lot less intimidating than $1,000,000.

6 ~ Have Contingency Plans.

The only constant factor in life is change. If you're not ready for something you'll lose time and heart in the struggle, but anything you're prepared for, you sail through. Contingency plans mean you have alternatives and strategies to deal with any eventuality that may arise. If investment property tenants fail to pay the rent or cause damage, owners panic. But if you've had the foresight to take out tenant insurance, know the procedures for eviction, have kept track of any lease infringements, or just have a reliable manager, it won't distract or cost you – because you were prepared and made your plans beforehand. If you put all your eggs in one basket and it does poorly, as superannuation (401[K] in America) did recently, you'll lose both money and sleep. But if you diversify your holdings and keep an eye on the markets, you won't be caught out.

> *'Everybody has a plan, until they get hit.'*
> ~ Mike Tyson ~

7 ~ Review Your Goals

It's prudent to review your goals on a regular basis. This not only lets you know how you're doing and keeps contingencies clear, but more importantly it keeps your goals in the forefront of your mind, where all important matters should be. Printing them out, carrying them with you, and reading them daily is a simple but very powerful way to remind yourself what you're doing, and why. What you think about, you bring about – so think about your dreams as much as possible and watch them become realities.

> *'Know that not easily shall a conviction arise in a man*
> *unless he every day speaks the same thing,*
> *and hear the same things,*
> *and at the same time apply them unto life.'*
> ~ Epictetus ~

Got it? Is that all clear? If you do this, your life cannot remain the same. And so you'll know that it's not just us making up a lot of hopeful instructions, in case your fiscal dog is still resisting his bath, this should remove any doubt from your mind and start you planning.

There were over 1,000 students in the Yale University graduating class of 1953, and as sociological study was popular in the 50s, they were asked a series of questions. One of the questions was, 'Do you have clear, specific financial goals, and do you have a written plan for achieving those goals?' and the answers were recorded for later analysis.

Only 3% of the class answered 'yes' to that particular question. Twenty years later, in 1973, the researchers completed their study by interviewing the surviving members of the 1953 class. Collating the information afterwards, they were amazed to find that the combined wealth of the 3% who'd written down their financial goals and detailed plans was greater than the entire remaining 97% put together!

This story has been told and retold for over 40 years by the world's top inspirational speakers such as Zig Ziglar, Mark Victor Hansen, and Dr John Demartini, because it is such compelling evidence for the power of a plan. Successfully used as a motivating tool for generations, there's one more surprising aspect to this tale – it never actually happened. Someone finally researched the university records, and found that no such study or follow-up was ever done. The unknown creator used it to inspire people into action, because he knew the importance of planning.

Many urban beliefs are lies wrapped in apparent truth, but this story is the opposite – a great truth wrapped in a myth. Like a fable, the story was made up to carry the message that a detailed plan will utterly transform your wealth, and your life. The details are secondary, the truth stands. IT WORKS, if you work it!

'Successful people do the things today that other people don't like to do, so they can have the things other people won't have tomorrow.'
~ John Hanna ~

~ EXERCISE ~

This whole chapter was actually an exercise, and this is an extension of it. We described the importance of being able to see a plan with your mind's eye, and now you're going to see it with your physical eyes – the Dream Board is a powerful tool to bring your inner vision into the world.

Get a big corkboard and a box of drawing pins, a pile of magazines, and a pair of scissors. Then go through the magazines and cut out every picture that reflects your vision. Houses, chalets, golf courses, cars, boats, planes, piles of cash, mounds of gold, beautiful clothes, jewellery, magnificent gardens, works of art, holiday resorts from around the world… if it inspires you, take it.

When you have your pictures, don't just stick them up and forget about it. Arrange them on the board with care, and put it where it's the first thing you see in the morning and the last thing you see at night. The purpose is to remind and inspire you, and to make it not just an aspiration but a reality, here and now.

Now, this is the crucial part: it's important that this wealth is not just there in the abstract, but linked in your perceptions to your own life. Take photos of yourself of the appropriate size, and put them onto your dream board as well. Now it's not just a beautiful house, but *your* beautiful house that you are standing on the lawn or in the doorway of; not just a luxury car, but *your* luxury car with your smiling face behind the wheel; not just a ski resort full of happy strangers, but *you* skiing and living that lifestyle, and so on.

Don't underestimate the power of any form of vision. Seeing yourself with great wealth, even in miniature, speaks to your unconscious and says that it's possible. Anything you see and hear enough, you will believe, so take charge of your input. The masses say, 'Seeing is believing,' and only believe something after it exists. The masters believe first, and then it becomes visible. This chapter is a big step in helping you believe that you can become wealthy.

'You hear a lot these days;
"Never let go of your dream!"
which is all very well,
I suppose – it's a bit too Walt Disney for me.
But if you really believe something,
there's a very good chance it will happen.
I always believed I'd be a comedian.'
~ Billy Connolly ~

PART TWO
OUTER WEALTH
~ DOING ~

Chapter 4

The Saving
You Are Worth It

*'It is not because things are difficult that we do not dare;
it is because we do not dare that they are difficult.'*
~ Seneca ~

In the first 3 chapters we explored the inner qualities and state of mind that are so vital in wealth creation – the *being*. Now we'll turn to the equally important physical actions – the *doing*. Remember, you need both spirit and matter working together to create real and lasting success.' As we've said, there are 7 things that successful people do which most aren't willing to face, and all 7 are vital. These laws may seem challenging at first, but how much harder is it to work for 50 years with nothing but a pension at the end of it all? You've already begun your transformation by valuing wealth, accepting personal responsibility for your life, and writing a financial plan. Now we'll continue this journey along the path to financial freedom by looking back in time.

Tithing is an ancient practice based on an understanding of how the real world works. It literally means 'a tenth part', and was originally called *first fruits*. In ages past, 10% of every harvest was put into a common holding for the whole village. They knew from experience that on average, 7% of the population could not work because they were either too old or too young or injured or ill, and 3% of the crop would be lost due to weather, pests, and spoilage. Having the foresight to save that 10% ensured survival through winter, disease, and famine. Later on when the church and state separated into separate powers, both took their tithe, and taxation grew from there.

'The art of taxation consists in so plucking the goose as to obtain the largest possible amount of feathers with the smallest possible amount of hissing.'
~ Jean-Baptiste Colbert ~ 1665

The tithe was imposed by superior powers – the village, state, or church – for a bigger purpose, and now you're going to assume that power over yourself. As part of taking responsibility for your life, *tithe your earnings* by giving *yourself* 10% of everything you earn. This is something that the wealthy have always done, it's the quickest way to become one of them, and we're going to show you how. It may seem challenging at first, like all new disciplines, but no-one honest ever said getting rich was going to be easy. The easy thing would be to spend it all and let the future take care of itself. The following tale illustrates how that story ends.

Fables hold deeper truths hidden in a story, and one tells of the grasshopper and the ant. All summer long the ant laboured, gathering and storing food, while the grasshopper played the fiddle and mocked him for working so hard.

'There is plenty of food, why not enjoy life? Come and sing with me,' he cried, as the ant passed by with yet another load of food.

The ant replied, 'And what will you do when winter comes, foolish creature?' and went back to work.

*But the grasshopper merely laughed and continued to play. Slowly but surely the summer passed, then the autumn, and both lived according to their own nature. When winter finally came, as it must, the grasshopper perished with the first frost, while the ant stayed snug below ground with his family and food all around him. You probably know many human grasshoppers and ants, but have you considered which one **you** are?*

The rich and poor have entirely different philosophies around wealth; the rich *invest* their money first and spend what is left, while the poor *spend* their money first and invest what is left, which is usually nothing. Self-tithing is a big step on the road to a wealthy future, because it says you're worth more than any other bill or expense. Saving and investing is a form of honouring yourself. The rich pay themselves first, the poor pay themselves last, and that's *why* they both are where they are. This is the basis for the third law of finance:

Financial Law ~ 3 ~
Save 10% Of Everything You Earn

What this means is quite simple. Gross earnings are how much money you make, while net earnings are how much you have left after taxes and expenses. You've already done the hard part, which is making the money in the first place. All you do now is take 10% of your *gross* earnings and put it into a savings account. From now on, before you spend a dollar on *anything*, you save. No matter how much or how little you make, skim off the first 10% into savings, because the richness is always in the cream on the top. But unless you understand the power of saving, you'll find this very difficult to do.

You must value wealth for it to come to you. If it's not high enough on your value list, you will never have any savings, which was the purpose for the linking exercise in Chapter 1. Like time, money is spent according to values, so if your top values were children, family, and home, that's where your money will automatically go, with little or nothing left over for savings. Because you're taking this 10% off the top and doing it first, that means saving is now your highest value, and it gets done *no matter what*.

What's probably going through your mind right now is; '**What?** I'm *barely making ends meet now, and you're telling me I'm going to have to get by on 10% **less?**! No way, it's just not possible.'* But let's look at it another way and see if that's actually true. If your employer announced tomorrow that the company was in trouble and everyone would have to take a 10% wage cut, would you survive? Of course you would – somehow you'd make it work, because you had to.

And most people can save for a new car or holiday or TV, but when it's a matter of discipline rather than indulgence, suddenly it's all just too hard. But that's a myth, because they've already done it for their higher values. If your job or desire for a new toy make you do it, you survive. But if *you* make yourself do it, for a purpose, you prosper. The easy line of least resistance, spending it all, comes with a huge long-term cost.

The average American saves .7% of their income.
93% rely on social security in retirement,
and 67% of them also require family assistance.

No matter what stage of life you're at, you'll have excellent reasons why you can't save right now – and none of them are true. How many of these excuses have you used?

Age 18 – 25

I can't save *now*! I'm just getting started in life. God knows I don't make much, and I deserve a little fun while I'm young. Clothes and going out cost a lot, and I need a car to get around in, but there's plenty of time. I'll wait until I'm making a bit more, then start saving.

Age 25 – 35

I can't save *now*! The car registration is due, and the brakes have had it. I've got a growing family, and the kids and house cost a fortune. It takes everything I've got to keep them going, but when they're older it will cost less. I'll save then.

Age 35 – 50

I can't save *now*! I've got two kids in high school and they think I'm made of money. It's all I can do to cover their expenses, I even had to borrow to cover the tuition last year. We're trying to pay off the mortgage, the car tyres are nearly bald, and we need a holiday. This is the most expensive time of life – I can't save a penny!

Age 50 – 65

I can't save *now*! I know I should, but things just aren't going well at the moment. It's hard for someone my age to change jobs, the old car needs constant repairs, our medical expenses are way up, the kids need help with their mortgages, and the money just doesn't go far enough. I'll just ride along where I am, maybe something will break, but I *certainly* can't save now.

Age 65

Well, I *can't* save now, I have no job. We're living with my son and his wife, my pension is barely enough to survive on, and my only asset is my vintage car. I wish I'd started saving 40 years ago, but it's too late now.

Virtually everyone agrees that it all makes perfect sense; they know they should be saving, they've seen what happened to their parents and grandparents, and they're definitely going to start. *Unfortunately* it's just not possible at the moment – but when they make more money they'll start immediately. The word 'un-fortunately' is accurate, because those who don't save rob themselves of a potential fortune. Nobody believes it will happen to them until it does, and by then it's too late to do anything about it.

This blindness is the result of herd instinct, thinking that as long as we do what everyone else does we'll be okay. A story from the old Wild West reveals the flaw in that reasoning. Before 1830, bison covered North America in vast herds as far as the eye could see, and their population was estimated at 20-30 *million* huge creatures. By 1889 there were exactly 1,091 animals left and they were on the brink of extinction. How did this happen? It wasn't just the number of hunters, it was the behaviour of the bison themselves. They were so complacent that the hunters could shoot into a herd until they ran out of ammunition, and those left standing would simply go on grazing! The buffalo ignored what was going on all around them, thinking it couldn't happen to them until it did.

Don't keep doing the human financial equivalent of grazing, ignoring the facts until it's too late. You may think you can't save until you have more money, but the truth is just the opposite – until you save, you *won't* have more.

> ### 'How much money does the average man need to be happy? Just a little bit more.'
> ~ Nelson Rockefeller ~

A financial study in the late 1990s asked people earning $40,000 and $100,000 and $400,000 a year how much more they'd need to be free from financial stress. All three groups gave the same answer – *"About another 10% should do it. If we had that, we'd be fine."*

Saving 10% – the power of it goes far beyond the increasing dollar amounts, valuable as they are. Savings and discipline increase your self-worth, which is *magnetic*, and your net worth automatically follows it. The moment you make a stand for something greater than immediate gratification, the world responds by increasing the amount of money that comes to you. But if *you* don't, *it* won't.

> ### 'Until you can manage your money wisely, don't expect more money to manage.'
> ~ Dr John F. Demartini ~

If you're not doing your job well, do you get promotions or more responsibility? Of course not; companies don't reward incompetent employees, and neither does the universe. It's a very efficient system, and doesn't waste resources. If you can't handle what you've got, why would it give you more? Overspending is gross mismanagement, and automatically limits the amount of money you're given to manage. But when you say to yourself and the world, 'I am worthy of this', and prove it by having the discipline to save, you automatically attract more. If you mismanage your money it will leave you, but order and organisation are forces that attract even more. By organising your finances this way, money will be drawn to you.

> ### 'Until you can manage your emotions, don't ever expect to be able to manage money.'
> ~ Warren Buffet ~

The test of your commitment is this; that you never, never, *never* spend your savings. And you will definitely be tested – three times. First from within by having to resist your own impulse to spend them; 'Just this once, because this bill is important,' or, 'This is a great buy.' Then you'll be tested from without by your partner; 'Because we/I really need this. Don't you love me?' And finally you'll be tested by the world; something completely unexpected will arise to tempt you, to make sure *you're* sure. Forewarned is forearmed – we tell you this so you'll recognise the tests when they appear, and be stronger in your determination not to give in to them.

Tim ~ Part II

A client came to me in early 1999 and said, "I've been working for 10 years now and I have no savings. I spend all I earn, and I've just realised that unless I change, I'm going to end up with nothing. I know you deal with emotional stuff, but can you help me with this?"

So I spent an hour with her going over the 10% multi-leveled sav-ings plan (which we'll develop in the next chapter), *and at the end she said, "Is **that** all it takes? That's easy! Thanks very much." I reminded her about the three tests, she gave a cheerful little nod, and happily went off to start being wealthy.*

I didn't hear from her for about a year and a half, and then one day she called for another appointment. The young woman I saw that day was not at all cocky, she was quiet and quite humbled. I asked her how it had been going, and this is what she said.

"Your advice seemed so easy, I was sure I could do it standing on my head, and for three months I saved 10% without fail. It felt pretty good, but then the clutch went in my car and it wasn't worth fixing. I was really glad to have the savings then and got a new one, but I felt a little odd when I took it all out of the bank. Kind of disappointed in myself, but it wore off and I started saving again.

"Three months later my savings were back up, but then my boyfriend told me immigration was after him and without a good lawyer he'd be deported. Of course he had no money, so I 'borrowed' from my savings again to help him, and this time I wasn't just disappointed, I was de-pressed. All that saving and I had nothing again, so now I was really determined.

"I saved really hard for nine months, much more than 10% to make up for what I'd lost, and had $17,000 in the bank. It felt so good, and I was so proud of myself for sticking with the discipline, and then..."

I gave her a tissue to wipe her eyes, and she sighed and went on;
"Then I met this really smart stockbroker who said my returns were ridiculously low, and that I was missing out on great opportunities to make some real money. He said timing was crucial and I had to act now, so I did. I gave him all my savings to invest, and for a couple of months I

made much more than the bank rate, and it felt fantastic! Then 9/11 hit, and the market crashed, and of course my stocks were the worst to have, and I lost almost everything. I was way past depressed, I was tired and angry and so upset, and then I remembered the three tests. So here I am again, can you help me?"

I reassured her that she wasn't alone, or foolish, that I'd done the same, and that was exactly how we learn. I asked, "Have you got it now?" and she just nodded her head. "Are you going to be fooled by any temptations again, now that you know how it feels?" and she shook her head vehemently. "Well, congratulations, that was your apprenticeship. Now you're ready to start saving."

We went over the principles again, and off she went. She called me a few years later to say that her savings were stable and growing, and nothing could break her discipline now; she had saved $70,000 and was about to buy her first home. So you can choose to listen to us, and to her, and save yourself the painful lessons, or you can go through the whole process yourself. Either way, you can't lose; one path just takes a little longer.

If you do give in to temptation (which is perfectly normal; remember, this is a well-trodden path you're on), you'll feel bad about it and beat yourself up a bit, mourn the hard-earned savings, and next time you'll be more disciplined.

If you don't give in, no matter what, some very odd things will happen. When you get a bill you don't think you can pay, but still refuse to rob your savings, time and again the money will magically appear at the last moment. From some completely unexpected source, it will come; you'll be offered more work, or a pay rise, someone will repay a debt, you'll find a forgotten nest egg, or a tax return will arrive, but somehow the bill will be paid. When it happens you'll begin to trust the principle, become more certain, and even more wealth will come to you. So either way, by giving in or staying strong, you're being trained to save.

> *'Conquering others requires force.*
> *Conquering oneself requires strength.'*
> ~ Lao Tzu ~

The point is – Save! The amounts don't matter, it's the *habit*. Get the habit and the money will grow. What does your computer ask you to do every time you finish work? Save! The message is all around us if we only pay attention. Historically, far more money has been made through saving than speculation or investment – it's a simple mathematical formula. You can only work so many hours a day or week, but money never sleeps; it works for you 24 hours a day, 365 days a year, and the more you have the more it makes. Those who devalue money, who don't honour it, spend their entire lives working for it – they are its slave. Those who value money eventually have it working for them – they become its master.

The goal is to eventually have your money make more than you can earn by working. At that point you become free; you no longer *have* to do anything, and can do what you would love. Ultimately, wealth is nothing less than freedom.

> *'If you want to become really wealthy,*
> *you must have your money work for you.*
> *The amount of money you get paid for*
> *your personal effort is small compared to the amount*
> *you can earn by having your money make money.'*
> ~ John D. Rockefeller ~

And here's another hidden aspect to saving. Have you noticed that no matter how much money you make, your expenses always expand to match your income? Most people, whatever they earn, always seem to end up with more month at the end of their money than money at the end of the month. But you can break free of this dead-end cycle by understanding the law of Supply and Demand. Supply, the available amount of anything, increases when the demand for it increases, and as demand goes down, so does supply. Most people just manage to pay their bills; that is, their *supply* of money exactly covers the *demands* they put on it, with little or nothing left over. This law has been working against you, but we're going to show you how to turn it to your advantage.

Have you ever been caught short and facing embarrassment or even eviction from your home, and somehow came up with the cash? Or perhaps you were about to miss a payment and lose your car, and even though it seemed impossible, you found the money somewhere. What actually happened was that your financial demand on yourself went up, and you automatically responded by creating more supply. If you don't put a demand on yourself, you'll always break even, because supply and demand always balance or *equilibrate* each other.

But in a crisis the game changes, and so do you – the difference is *urgency*. When you really need something, you make it happen, and increasing the demand on yourself is a great way to create urgency. A colleague of ours once worked with an American businessman who makes the clothes for the world's top fashion houses in his numerous Chinese factories. He has to run it all; make sure all the orders are filled and on time, every season's products are perfect, and manage over 15,000 employees. When asked the secret of his incredible productivity he said, *"Everything is effing urgent!"*

Have you also noticed that while your expenses tend to expand to match your income, on the other side your income grows to meet your expenses? Instead of fighting the law of supply and demand, why not use it to make you more money? In addition to your rent or mortgage, car payment, credit cards, health insurance, and all the rest, simply create another payment – *me*. Instead of believing that you don't have the money to save and ignoring it, treat it just like any other bill that you somehow manage to pay. Write down a figure equal to 10% of your income, put it in your bills folder, and pay it every month just like you do all the others. It's a small sacrifice with huge rewards.

> *'If you want a place in the sun,*
> *you have to expect a few blisters.'*
> ~ Loretta Young ~

There is a hierarchy of bills to pay, determined by their penalties, and it's best to pay them in order of penalty. If one bill has a late fee of $50 and another has none, which one should you pay first? The penalised one, of course. But what most people don't grasp is that the bill with the highest penalty, and the greatest reward, is *yourself*. If you don't honour and respect yourself enough to save, the loss of self-worth and opportunities and wealth is the highest price of all.

And when you pay a bill, don't resent it. Be grateful for the product or service you've bought, and that you have the money to pay for it. When money flows from you with gratitude, it flows to you much more easily.

The order in which to pay bills is: self first, then taxes (because they carry such heavy penalties), then living and business expenses – the last two by priority of penalty. It's also smart to set up a tax account and make deposits there on a monthly or quarterly basis, otherwise you'll resent them for taking 'your' money. This way you not only avoid financial pressure at tax time, you collect interest on 'their' money throughout the year. When you have no resentment it's easier to pay, and it's unwise to resent a government, because it's a higher power than you.

Understand that the amounts will start small, but they'll become larger and larger over time. You'll also experience an unexpected development; as soon as your savings reach a certain level, which varies with each person, they suddenly become your highest priority. The satisfaction and sense of achievement you get from seeing them grow will be far greater than any other use of your money, and your confidence and sense of self-worth will grow along with it.

Earlier we talked about people managing to buy luxuries but being unable to save. If you want to buy something large or special and aren't sure if you should, or if you can afford it – here's the test. If you can afford to put the same amount extra into your savings as the thing costs, you can afford it. That means you must come up with twice the purchase price in order to buy something; in this way you'll not only avoid financial irresponsibility, it will actually help you save faster!

When supermodel Kate Moss was asked where she found the discipline to control her weight over such a long career, she replied, "Nothing tastes as good as thin feels," and to paraphrase her, no buying spree or 'retail therapy' will ever feel as good or empowering as real wealth. Anyone who's ever lost weight or gained wealth knows that both take discipline – and both are worth it.

Another hidden benefit to saving lies in the fact that the average person has unexpected bills of about $300 per month – this form of depreciation is a physical/financial expression of entropy, the tendency of matter to break down or wear out. It also manifests as medical expenses, tooth decay, car repairs, traffic fines, etc. But if you put at least half that amount extra into your savings, you'll see those unexpected bills drop. It's the universe's way of encouraging you to save, but don't just take our word – try it and see.

Here's another slightly spooky aspect to saving. If you have an ongoing payment, say for a car, the moment the debt is paid off put that exact amount into your savings. If you don't, either your income will drop or your expenses will increase to match it. You were already able to make the payment before, so it's no hardship, and instead of loss of income you turn it into an increase in savings.

Also, there's no such thing as a fixed income without a fixed mind. If you save and invest, within three to five years you will no longer be on a fixed income. That alone can extend your life; self-employed men are 57% less likely to die from *all* causes than men who take orders from others, and if your income is in the top 20% you'll live, on average, six years longer than the bottom 20%.

Don't underestimate the power of this practice – it's how the wealthy of the world got where they are today. If you apply nothing else from this entire book, valuable as it all is, this one act will change your life. What starts as challenging becomes effortless, and the gains far exceed the cost. Estimate how much you've earned so far in your working life, and imagine you had 10% of it in the bank right now. How would you feel about yourself and your life? What are you doing today that you would stop immediately, and what would you be free to do that you'd love?

Most people say they'll start saving when they have more to save, which is a prescription for poverty. Those who don't want to think about such things but 'just live' will get their wish and end up living – on social security, and that is nobody's highest dream.

If you don't pay yourself first, why would anyone else? You attract people into your life to pay you in direct proportion to how *you* pay you. If you wait and pay yourself last, so will the world. The best time to start saving is yesterday, the next best time is today, and the worst time is tomorrow; time is crucial, and the longer you save the more wealth you will have. Of course it takes courage and will, but isn't that the way with anything of lasting value?

'Courage is not the absence of fear, but rather the judgment that something else is more important than fear.'
~ Ambrose Redmoon ~

~ Exercise ~

So how do you start receiving all these marvellous and almost too-good-to-be-true benefits? Simply go to your bank and arrange to have a weekly or monthly *automatic 10% withdrawal* of all income deposits from your account into a special savings account. We call it the 'immortality account' because it's an investment in your future and that of your descendants, so it goes beyond your life. It helps to think of any money deposited there as no longer yours, but as belonging to your future, your children, or *their* children – if you don't own it, you're much less likely to spend it.

Make sure the account has the highest interest and lowest fees available, and if your bank doesn't have all three components; high interest, low fees, and automatic withdrawal, change banks. If your income fluctuates, nominate 10% or a set figure, whichever is highest. This will not only grow your savings faster, it'll also stabilise and increase your income.

Why automatic withdrawal? Because of human nature. Decades of research have found that if life insurance payments are auto-debited, after five years 93% of policies are maintained, but if cheques have to be written or money transferred, the figure drops to 69%. If you leave it discretionary, that is, up to you, you'll be tempted and waver and lose discipline. By making it automatic you take out the emotional factor, and eventually you don't even notice it.

No one in the history of finance has ever found a single logical reason not to save. The very worst thing that can happen is you'll have the money when you need it, and the best is that you become wealthy and free to live the life you'd love – it's a clear and simple choice, but it's still up to you.

Save your money now, and one day it will save you.

> ### *'If you can't run with the big dogs, don't get off the porch.'*
> ~ Dr. Phil ~

Chapter 5

The Pyramid
Building for the Ages

'I don't know much about being a millionaire,
but I bet I'd be darling at it.
~ Dorothy Parker ~

Now that you've set in train the processes which will create wealth for you, it's important to be able to manage it when it arrives. It's a very common fantasy that being poor is hard, while being wealthy is a free ticket to easy street with nothing to do but sit back and let your accountants do the work. In fact, nothing could be further from the truth. Just ask legendary musician Leonard Cohen, who had to go back on the road at age 70 because a trusted business manager stole his life savings of $6,000,000; or the artist Ken Done who invested $58,000,000 – his entire fortune – with a major Australian bank and was devastated to find that more than $50,000,000 had been thrown away on bizarre speculative investments; or Ireland's once richest man, Sean Quinn, worth US $6 billion in 2008, and declared bankrupt in January 2012 owing $4.5 billion because he unwisely invested it all in one bank that collapsed. There are countless examples of people who worked a lifetime to amass a fortune, only to have it vanish almost overnight because they failed to take proper care of it.

Would you know how to fix your car's engine without training and experience? Well, skilful wealth management is a *lot* more complex than car repair. We've said that power and responsibility go hand in hand, and the great power of wealth carries an equal responsibility to manage it. If you don't know much about it, if you're not a financial genius yourself, you'd better make darned sure that the people you entrust your money to *are*, or you're asking for trouble. We know one successful man who made over $6,000,000 one year, then had to borrow $200,000 to pay his taxes. Why? Because he doesn't know how to manage it.

Having taken four steps on the path – valuing wealth, accepting responsibility, writing a plan, and saving 10% – you've come a long way already. The next big question is what to do with the stuff as it starts to accumulate. That means investment, and *where* you invest is a vital part of your entire wealth creation strategy. Viable investments should fulfill certain basic requirements: they should be safe, work around the clock, produce an income, and multiply in value over time.

But how do you accomplish this complex and demanding task? It seems like a catch-22, because if you *knew* how to do it you'd already be wealthy – but there is a way. The first thing to do is make sure you get the right advice, and this book is an excellent start. Do not be misled by people who don't truly know what they're talking about, 'experts' without a proven track record, or the advice of well-meaning but uninformed friends. If they aren't successful themselves in that area, you're playing against some very long and unfriendly odds. Here is an excellent illustration of the importance of the right advice from one of the classic works on wealth creation.

My own investment was a tragedy to me at the time. The guarded savings of a year I did entrust to a brick-maker named Azur who was travelling over the far seas to Tyre, and agreed to buy for me the rare jewels of the Phoenicians. These we would sell upon his return and divide the profits. The Phoenicians were scoundrels and sold him bits of glass. My treasure was lost. Today, my training would show to me at once the folly of entrusting a brick-maker to buy jewels.

Therefore, do I advise from the wisdom of my experiences: be not too

confident of thine own wisdom in entrusting thy treasures to the possible pitfalls of investments. Better by far to consult the wisdom of those experienced in handling money for profit. Such advice is freely given for the asking and may readily possess a value equal in gold to the sum thou considerest investing. In truth, such is its actual value if it save thee from loss.
~ George Clayson ~ 'The Richest Man in Babylon'

Given the complexity of the modern world, this advice is all the more valid today. Even though you may feel you know exactly what you're doing, it's far wiser to learn first, and act second. You can learn by personal experience and trial and error – which works, although it's painful and costly in both time and money, or you can stand on the shoulders of giants and benefit from centuries of *other* people's trials and errors. Why reinvent the wheel when it's already there, waiting to take you where you want to go?

'Experience is a hard teacher because it gives the test first, and the lesson afterwards.'
~ Vernon Law ~

This chapter will set out a safe, reliable investment strategy that has stood the test of time. Neither a fad nor a fashion, it has worked successfully throughout the history of wealth, and we'll introduce it by going a little aside to reveal the fourth universal principle:

Universal Principle ~ 4 ~
All Life is a Hierarchy

This principle pervades all of life, and we can see it most immediately in our own bodies. From sub-atomic particles, through atoms and molecules to cells, tissues, organs and organ systems to the whole body, we're a network of interconnected levels of increasing complexity. If any of the lower levels are out of order, the whole system breaks down.

Physically, there's also a normal developmental process for children; from lying on their back to rolling onto their stomach, then raising their

59

head and looking around, sitting up, then crawling, standing, walking, and eventually running. If any stage is missed or incomplete, learning and developmental difficulties occur later and the child has to go back and relearn them in the proper order.

Finance itself has evolved through a hierarchy of ever-greater complexity and speed. Originally wealth was based on cattle (the term 'capital' comes from *caput* or 'head' of livestock), and any movement of wealth entailed long and hazardous cattle drives with much loss along the way. This cumbersome system was improved by the invention of letters of credit that could be exchanged for equivalent numbers of cattle. Next came the breakthrough to currency, first as coins and then notes, then credit cards, and now we have completely paperless systems based on the electronic transfer of data. In both our bodies and in finance, increasingly sophisticated levels are built on earlier forms.

So what does all this have to do with investment? *Everything*. Remember we said that universal laws have great power because the universe itself uses them on every level of existence? Well, the more your investment strategy follows natural growth patterns, the more reliable and effective it will be. Without all the intermediate steps, your body would be unstable, and so will your investments.

The pyramids of Egypt are the only survivors of the 7 wonders of the ancient world. As the most enduring edifice on earth, the pyramid represents both financial and universal principles, and is a model for growth and stability. Life evolves through hierarchies, and so should your wealth. Now you can see how this universal law links to the fourth law of finance:

Financial Law ~ 4 ~
Select The Right Investment

The more money you have, the more important it becomes to know how to invest and manage it properly. Otherwise, at best you'll miss opportunities for growth, and at worst you could lose it all. To avoid the pitfalls, build a financial structure that will guide and protect you through the snares that await the innocent, the ignorant, and the reckless.

Warren Buffet, the billionaire investment guru, says that the number one obstacle to wealth is emotions, and the more emotional your financial decisions are the less reliable they'll be. Fear and greed are the great saboteurs of wealth, and should have no place in your decision-making process. Emotions are not creative or strategic, they're *reactive*. They have no patience, they need results *now*, and those who try to make it rich quick usually end up being wiped out instead. Great at jumping on bandwagons, following herds over cliffs, and panicking at obstacles and challenges, emotions are the worst possible directors of your financial destiny. Millionaires whose fortunes last are methodical and consistent. They have a long-term plan and stick to it, so if you want to join them, do what they do.

> **'Control your emotion, or it will control you.'**
> ~ Samurai Proverb ~

So our first step is to take emotions out of the equation. Emotions are caused by two things – having too much, or having too little. When we have too much of something desirable we get elated, when we have too little we get depressed, and both are major distractions and energy drains. We'll deal with the second cause now, and the 'problem' of too much money (sounds like a nice change, doesn't it?) we'll address in the final chapter. In any area of life, if we don't have enough – air, or water, or food, or time, or space, or money – we first become stressed, then start to panic, and in that state we tend to make unwise decisions very quickly. We're now going to introduce you to an investment plan that is simple, doable, and which removes any impulse to react emotionally.

If a child tries to run before they can walk, or walk before they can crawl, it creates problems for them. We grow in stages, and it's the same with finances; it's actually quicker to build a stable base and make haste slowly from there. If you try to leap ahead of your abilities, you'll end up falling back to the level you've actually mastered. That means if someone comes along with a 'hot tip' that's going to make you a pile of money, one of two things will probably happen. The first and most likely is that you will simply lose all your money immediately. The second possibility is that you'll make money, get elated, mismanage it, and lose it later. Either way, the result is the same – you exchanged your money for financial and emotional lessons.

> *'The safest way to double your money is to fold it over and put it in your pocket.'*
> ~ Kin Hubbard ~

But if you build your base first, you'll be emotionally stable enough to handle market fluctuations; you'll have earned the right to be there through discipline and patience in your strategy. Those who manage their money well are automatically given more money to manage, and those who don't are given lessons. You gain something no matter what you do, but if you prefer cash to lessons, here's how.

The Investment Pyramid

Level One

We're going to start out building your financial structure simply, and along the way you'll learn to manage money, minimise your emotions, and earn the right to higher risks and returns. The first stage is to create a purely cash account at 4-6% interest, and keep depositing the magical 10% until it reaches the equivalent of 60 days of your income. This is the 'immortality account' you began after the last chapter, and now we're just linking it into a bigger plan and picture. If you already have savings, you can distribute them into the various levels we'll describe and have a good head start.

Experts advocate between 30 and 90 days of income per level, so we recommend the 60 day average between their extremes. That means if you make $10,000 a month you want $20,000 in this account, if you make $50,000 it should contain $100,000 and so on, either more or less depending on your income. This is your liquid reserve – you don't touch it, but it's available just in case. Again, choose a bank with the best interest and lowest fees.

Some might object, "But I could make a hell of a lot more than that in property, or the stock market!" but that's not the *point*. The purpose of this account is not to maximise returns, because it's not actually an investment – it's *savings* to build your emotional stability, and the more you have, the more emotionally stable you'll be. It increases your self worth, and remember that *that's* what raises your net worth. Keep making regular deposits into this account until you reach 60 days of income, then you're ready for the next stage.

Level Two

This is a slightly higher rate of return, but still very safe. Here you want to get 6-8%, which is available through fixed-term deposits, bonds, or treasury bills in the U.S. market. It's a little less liquid, with moderate yield, and still stable and secure. You don't encounter real risk until after 8% – once you pass that number you're into investment, before that it's just called savings. Again, keep making your regular 10% deposits here until you reach the equivalent of 60 days' income.

Level Three

Now that you've built your first two levels you can look for an 8-10% return, and this can be achieved through such vehicles as a managed fund (mutual fund in the U.S.), or property. Here is where you'd begin to seek advice from a financial consultant. Again, build to 60 days worth of your income. You should be able to get your first property with a down payment of 10-20% of the purchase price, depending on whether or not you take out mortgage insurance. If that's a little more than your 60 days income, extend your savings time until you have it.

If your property is positively geared – which means that the rent exceeds your mortgage and other costs so you're making money – leave the excess in an account to service that property, just in case. If your property is negatively geared – ie, your costs are greater than the rent – then the loss is a tax deduction, so it's saving you money as it appreciates in value over time. In this case, maintain an interest-bearing account to service the property, and top it up as necessary. Eventually, it will become positively geared and you can leave it to take care of itself, and use the equity or value in it to buy another.

Some people are happy to stop building up here and go lateral, diversifying their holdings at this level because they don't trust the stock market. They feel more comfortable with bricks and mortar that they can see and touch, and which are less reactive to the world economy. If that sounds like you, this will be your strategy, and you can always choose to continue building higher at any time in the future. Certainly property is one of the oldest and most stable forms of wealth.

When William the Conqueror invaded England in 1066 he suddenly owned a whole new country, which meant revenue through taxation. He commissioned the most detailed accounting ever of a nation's wealth, 'The Domesday Book', which listed every chicken, cow, field, house, manor, and castle in England, with all their worth itemised. As a result, we know that property has increased in value by an average of 10% per year for the last thousand years. That's a pretty reliable statistic to keep in mind.

Level Four

You want 10-12% at this level, which you can get from a large cap stock – that means blue-chip companies with large capitalisation (ie, lots of money) and a proven history. They're the most stable, steady, reliable market investments. They don't have big swings that gain and lose vast amounts of money; they don't take risks because they don't have to, and know it's poor strategy.

Level Five

Here you can get 12-14% with mid-cap company stocks – they're a little more volatile, but you've earned the right to invest here and by now it's only a small percentage of your portfolio. The smaller the capitalisation of a company the more volatile it is, just like a person. That's why some of them gain and lose so much money, and come and go so quickly.

Five stages to your pyramid will take you many years into the future, and build a significant base of wealth. Once you've filled each successive level, stop depositing into it and go on to the next, but allow the interest to remain and grow in each stage. Many companies have a dividend reinvestment plan, which means that instead of getting a dividend cheque you're automatically issued more shares in the company at a reduced rate. And as your income increases (which it will do if you stay on track), go back and increase each level to match it and maintain 60 days' income. The first level may take a while, but each one is progressively quicker because the interest rates increase as you rise. Can you see how the structure of the pyramid reflects the third universal principle we shared with you, the One and the Many?

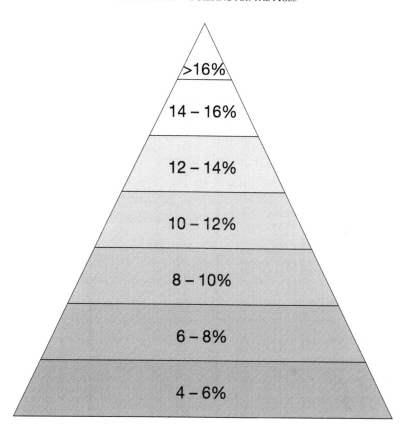

Pyramid of Savings

As your wealth increases, it's important to understand that you're an *investor*, not a speculator, and the difference between them is critical. Investors are in for the long term, while speculators are looking for a quick killing. You're not there to nervously watch the market and react to every twitch, jump, or fall it will inevitably make. Buy good quality stocks and stay with them. Don't sell sound stocks, because throughout the history of the stock market, it has always recovered from any loss and risen higher. The 'Great Depression' of 1929 created more millionaires than at any time in U.S. history, because the smart investors had not only diversified their holdings, they had enough savings to buy huge amounts of devalued stocks at the very bottom of the market. Well-structured savings can protect you as well as create new opportunities.

The immortality account makes you more stable so you don't react, and it's not yours anyway so you can just let it alone to do its work for you. If you have enough capital, as you will do if you follow this model, you'll be able to ride out any fluctuations. Only review and diversify your holdings in consultation with your financial adviser to take advantage of national and global trends and developments.

Later on you may want to create a sixth or seventh tier of 14-16% or more with small-cap companies, warrants, options, futures, art, etc. These are more specialised forms of exchange, but you'll have *earned* the right to be there because you've *learned* how to manage money. How high you want to go depends on your personal risk tolerance, but this is the structure you'd follow when relatively young. As you get older you may well become more conservative, and move your money back down the pyramid to where you feel comfortable, but it will ensure that you have money to move when you get there.

These 7 vertical tiers are called investment *classes*, and each successive one increases both the return and the risk, which is why you build them gradually – to increase your financial and emotional stability. To further reduce your risk, each vertical class can be broken up into several horizontal vehicles or *sectors*. The first two levels are about as safe as you can get, so diversification is not so vital here, but from levels three on up you don't want to have all your eggs in one financial basket.

Spread your investments across 3-7 different sectors – properties, shares, or funds. It's the nature of life to change, and money is no different. Diversifying in this way protects you if one of your vehicles fluctuates, because only a small part of your wealth is in any one of them. It protects you against loss and depression if one should go down, and it also protects you against elation should one sector or whole class have a major increase. As we've seen, elation and depression are the two great saboteurs of the wealth that you are now working not only hard, but also smart, to amass.

And remember, you do not touch this money – only in the most extreme emergency would you even consider it. It's not there to spend, but to stabilise your mind and your emotions so that your self-worth and confidence increase with your finances. If you have no savings you'll be more desperate and unstable, but with a reserve you'll be far more disciplined and consistent. Those who manage money are given more to manage, and those who methodically follow a slow strategy end up wealthier than those who don't. Patience trumps emotions every time.

If you have no savings and have a really *good* day or month or year, you'll get elated and sabotage your wealth. If you have no savings and have a really *bad* day, month, or year you'll get depressed, and guess what you'll do – that's right, sabotage your wealth again. With the emotions of either elation or depression, you don't run your life well. But if instead of nothing you have $100 in the bank you're a little less reactive, if you have $1,000 you're even less so, $10,000 less again, $100,000 less again, and if you have $1,000,000 in the bank, what effect does a big or little day have on you? None. In fact, you don't even notice it. The real power of money lies not in spending it, but in *having* it.

Your objective is to have your savings make more than you can earn by working. At 8%, savings of $1,000,000 will give you $80,000 a year in interest. $2,000,000 yields $160,000. $3,000,000 means $240,000. $4,000,000 gives you $320,000 and if you save $5,000,000 it will produce $400,000 every single year without you having to do anything. The more you have, the more you receive, and this principle isn't limited to interest alone.

Have you ever noticed that the less money you have, the more people and events seem to want to take it away from you? If you want to borrow money from a bank, the first thing they ask for is collateral – that is, something that can be converted into as much money as you want to borrow. But the reverse is also true; the richer you are, the more people want to give you money. When you're wealthy, banks want to lend you more, and offer you a better deal, because you're not a risk. If you already have $1,000,000 they're eager to lend you another million to get the interest – you just attract these people and events into your life because you're resonating at that level of finance.

Money is magnetic in proportion to its mass, and it plays a major role in the opportunities that come to you. If you have $100, you'll only attract $100 opportunities. If you have $1000 you attract $1000 opportunities, and $1,000,000 automatically attracts million-dollar opportunities into your life. It's a basic law, so the more disciplined you are in following your savings plan, not only will your wealth increase and your volatility shrink, but the opportunities that come to you will grow to match your savings. The more you *know*, the more you'll *have*, and the more will come to you.

> *'If ignorance is bliss,*
> *why aren't there more happy people in the world?'*
> ~ Stephen Fry ~

And when you do get advice, don't rely on just one person. People are fallible, and even those with high integrity and the best intentions don't know everything. Everyone has habits or fears that influence their behaviour, and you don't want to risk your hard-saved wealth on unknown factors. It's wise to learn from both sides of any equation, which in this case means taking advice from both an accountant *and* a financial adviser. Needless to say, both should be skilled and reputable, but they have very different approaches to money, and you want to use both of them.

Most accountants are by nature low-risk, cautious, conservative bean-counters. They're paid to protect wealth, not to grow it, so their focus is not to make money but to preserve what you have, without attracting the attention of the tax department – they're financial pessimists. The other side of the coin is the financial adviser; they're high-risk, adventurous speculators. They want to make a dramatic amount of money for you because they work on commission and referrals, so they're much less risk-averse than accountants – they're financial optimists. Input from both the number-crunching pessimist and the enthusiastic optimist will allow you to sit in the middle and be a realist, which is the ideal in money and in life.

We'd like to finish this very important chapter with a chilling little story that illustrates the importance of knowledge and patience, and reveals the cost of ignorance and emotion.

Lloyd's of London is a very old and respected underwriting firm which insures major projects and business ventures around the world, and since 1774 it has been making a great deal of money for its investors. In the early 1980s stories began to appear in the media about investors consistently receiving returns of 15-40%, sometimes in a matter of months, and the news triggered a financial feeding frenzy. People with no financial knowledge whatsoever, and who'd never invested in their lives, rushed to sink their life savings into this 'guaranteed gold mine'. Remember Bernard Baruch and the 1929 stock market crash? Well, that's also what they were calling the market then, so when you hear that phrase, stand well back and watch what happens.

Everything went reasonably well for a few years, and then came an unprecedented series of catastrophes. Hurricanes struck with extreme ferocity, ships and tankers were lost at sea, oil-drilling platforms were swept away, vast quantities of oil were spilled, the 1984 Bhopal pesticide plant disaster killed 11,000 people in India, and Lloyd's had insured them all. In the early 1990s they reported losses of £7.9 billion (US $12.4 billion). The new investors bore the brunt of these crushing losses, and they were wiped out by the tens of thousands.

What they didn't know was that they were not investing in the company itself, but in specific projects. Of course, the company gave the safest investments to their oldest clients, while the novices were allocated the high risk accounts. Across Great Britain, people suddenly found themselves not only bereft of their life savings and retirement funds, but also deeply in debt. They learned to their dismay that they'd lost not just their entire investment, but were also liable for the total payout on their allocated project, which could be three to four times their initial investment, and even more. As a result, countless investors lost their homes as well. When the story broke, through the same media that had reported the 'gold mine' in the first place, the hue and cry lasted for many weeks, and eventually a reporter was granted access to one of the firm's executives.

At the end of the interview, she finished by asking him a personal question; "Don't you feel any remorse for the thousands of mum and dad investors, all the little people who lost everything in this disaster?"

Now, this executive was due to retire, which may have been why he was given the onerous task of facing the press, but it also meant he wouldn't have to deal with any repercussions. Perhaps it was just his personality, or his mood on the day, but for some reason the man broke with corporate tradition and answered with complete honesty.

He looked directly at her and said, with what she described in her article as a 'wolfish gleam in his eye'; "If He hadn't meant them to be shorn, the good Lord wouldn't have made them sheep."

Callous? Yes. Cruel? Possibly. Accurate? Undeniably. Those unfortunate people were swept up in a tide of mass emotion, were looking for immediate and extreme profits, had no knowledge or experience of the market, did no research, and put all their eggs in one basket – the perfect formula for financial disaster. You work too hard for your money (you've actually traded a large part of your life for it), to throw it away with one poor decision.

The elated hysteria of the initial investment frenzy led directly to the crushing depression of losing it all and more. Emotions, friends, mass media, fads, luck, hunches, gambles, hope – none are good financial advisers, and for every one that succeeds there are a thousand that fail. Rely on history, proven strategies, and financial and universal laws to build a safe, steady, and reliable pyramid that will last your whole life and beyond.

~ EXERCISE ~

Remember we said that if you take every step with us you'll soon be in very different circumstances from those who merely read it? If you still haven't begun your 10% savings plan, do it now. That's Level One of this tried and tested financial strategy. We've just described how to build your investment pyramid, so simply follow the instructions for each successive level as you fill the one below.

All you need to do is begin, and commit yourself to it. It doesn't matter how much it is – the person who saves $100 or even $10 a month will eventually be wealthier than someone who makes a fortune and spends it all. The *habit* of saving is so much more important than the amount, because the amount will grow if you develop the habit. Eventually you'll realise that you don't even miss it. Those who wait until they have 'a little bit more' before they begin saving and never develop the habit are missing out on the most powerful wealth creation strategy of all time.

'If you want to create a miracle for yourself,
learn to get out of your own way.'
~ Carlos Santana ~

Chapter 6
The Compounding
Playing God

'If you should put even a little on a little,
and do this often,
soon this little would become big.'
~ Hesiod ~

In the last two chapters we introduced you to the concept and strategy of saving, and now we'll go even more deeply into the how and why of this powerful practice. Remember we said that those who work for money are its slaves, while those who have it work for them are its masters? Well, earning interest is the beginning of that process, but here is where the money really starts to work for you, because compounding means receiving interest on your interest. This chapter has some of those graphs and charts we promised not to overwhelm you with, but they're very simple and clear, with profound implications for your future.

Interest is a fascinating principle, but we haven't always been able to take advantage of this powerful tool. At one time the practice was banned throughout Christendom, for a somewhat bizarre reason. Originally called *usury*, it came to be regarded with horror because it caused money to multiply itself. To the modern mind, that's the whole point, but in the Middle Ages this was seen as a form of birth or procreation. Since only God had the power to create, usury was abhorred as a sacrilegious imitation of the power of divinity, damning the lender's immortal soul.

One unforeseen result of this ban was that business and commerce came to a grinding halt. Without interest to offset risk there was no motivation to lend and invest, without investment there was no trade, and without trade not only individuals but entire nations suffered. This disastrous state of affairs couldn't continue, but the Church couldn't recant its own dogma, so an alternative had to be found.

The solution took the form of non-Christian moneylenders, principally those of the Jewish faith, who had no such superstitious beliefs and could therefore lend money at interest without risking eternal damnation. Before the ban on usury was finally repealed, resentment over perfectly legal but 'unholy' debt created great prejudice and violence against those who performed this vital service. Rather than being demonised they should have been thanked, for they actually kept the world financially viable and evolving when it might otherwise have stagnated – but as always, wisdom lies not with the masses but with the masters. Fortunately, hellfire is no longer part of the deal, and this little history lesson brings us to the next financial law we have to share with you:

Financial Law ~ 5 ~
Utilise the Principle of Compounding

So we have interest today, but what does it mean? Put simply, interest is a fee paid for the use of your money, and compounding is the practice of receiving interest on your interest, which over time makes things extremely 'interesting'. In fact, it's one of the most powerful of all wealth creation principles. How does it work? Let's use an example to make this phenomenon perfectly clear. Say we were to offer you two choices:

Option 1 ~ You will receive $10,000 every day for 31 days.

Option 2 ~ You will receive 1¢ on the first day, to be doubled every day for 31 days.

Which one would you choose? Option 1 seems the obvious winner; it would give you $310,000 at the end of the month, and almost everyone (except the few who understand compounding) would choose it over merely multiplying an insignificant penny. Well, let's put it on a chart and see.

Days 1 — 10

Option 1		Option 2	
Day	$	Day	$
1	$10,000	1	$0.01
2	$10,000	2	$0.02
3	$10,000	3	$0.04
4	$10,000	4	$0.08
5	$10,000	5	$0.16
6	$10,000	6	$0.32
7	$10,000	7	$0.64
8	$10,000	8	$1.28
9	$10,000	9	$2.56
10	$10,000	10	$5.12
Total	$100,000	Total	$10.23

Option 2 is looking very unattractive right now.

Would you prefer to take the guaranteed $310,000 or keep compounding your $10.23 at 100% per day? Let's project even further.

Days 11 — 20

Option 1		Option 2	
Day	$	Day	$
11	$10,000	11	$10.23
12	$10,000	12	$20.46
13	$10,000	13	$40.92
14	$10,000	14	$81.84
15	$10,000	15	$163.68
16	$10,000	16	$327.36
17	$10,000	17	$654.72
18	$10,000	18	$1,309.44
19	$10,000	19	$2,618.88
20	$10,000	20	$5,237.76
Total	$200,000	Total	$10,475.52

Well, 20 days have passed, Option 2 is still only worth about 5% of Option 1, and there are just 11 days to go. Have you decided yet? Are you sure?

Days 21 — 31

Option 1		Option 2	
Day	$	Day	$
21	$10,000	21	$10,475
22	$10,000	22	$20,951
23	$10,000	23	$41,902
24	$10,000	24	$83,804
25	$10,000	25	$167,608
26	$10,000	26	$335,216
27	$10,000	27	$670,433
28	$10,000	28	$1,340,866
29	$10,000	29	$2,681,733
30	$10,000	30	$5,363,466
31	$10,000	31	$10,726,932
Total	$310,000	Total	$21,443,386

The choice is now a no-brainer, isn't it? Of course you won't be making 100% interest per day, but the principle holds true and clearly demonstrates the power of compounding, or the multiplication of interest over time. That's why it's so often referred to as 'the miracle of compound interest'. Known to the masters for many years, the masses are only dimly aware of its potential to create wealth.

This financial law blends seamlessly with the next universal principle:

Universal Principle ~5 ~
All Things Perish, Unless Something New is Added

Everything created is subject to a cycle of four stages – birth, maintenance, decay, and death. You can see it in your own body, which is born, matures and maintains itself, then gradually decays and eventually dies. This process applies to all of life: bacteria, buildings, companies, ideas, nations, planets, stars, and galaxies all follow the same pattern of four life stages. The ancient Hindus called it the Wheel of Life, or *Samsara*, and it's a fact of existence. It's how evolution works, by the extinction of old forms and the birthing of new ones, and you can't avoid it. However, it is possible to extend the maintenance phase almost indefinitely by giving new life and energy to existing structures, like putting more spin on a slowing wheel. Science calls it *negative entropy*, which means continued growth or evolution by the influx of new energy, and this principle can be used to create if not immortality, at least extended life and vitality for yourself and your wealth.

'People don't get old.
When they stop growing, they become old.'
~ Anonymous ~

A very old story shows how long this knowledge has been available to a chosen few.

To one of the ancient kingdoms of India, a sage came from a distant land and began speaking in the marketplace. His teachings held such wisdom that word quickly spread, and the Maharajah ('great king') ordered the man brought before him so that he too could receive these profound teachings. In the course of a single day the wise man imparted such knowledge to the ruler, and opened his eyes to so many hidden truths, that the king wished to reward him in proportion to the gifts he had bestowed so freely.

"What would you have of your Maharajah? Ask, and it shall be given with both hands."

The sage thought a moment and then said, "If it please your majesty, I am a humble man, and would be well satisfied with a little rice. I believe you play chess; would you be so kind as to place a single grain of rice on the first square of a board, two on the second, four on the third, and continue in like manner until all the squares are covered?"

The Maharajah was almost insulted at this reflection on his generosity and protested, "A handful of rice for such wisdom? Surely such precious gifts merit more from us than that," but the sage merely smiled and said, "Even so, that is all I require."

So the king reluctantly ordered that a chessboard be brought to the great hall and rice placed upon it to the instructions of the inscrutable sage. It indeed began with a single grain, but quickly grew to many sacks, then wagonloads, and eventually it became clear to the Maharajah that his entire kingdom did not contain enough rice to fulfill the contract, nor did all of India! He raised his eyes in astonishment to find the sage gently smiling and nodding, and realised that the man wanted no rice, but was still teaching. In an unprecedented act of humility the Maharajah descended from his throne to embrace the guest who had become his guru, and the sage remained with him for many years, instructing the king in the ways of nature and guiding the kingdom to peace and plenty.

So there we see the unquestionable power of multiplication linked to slow patient increase. Compounding actually relies upon two elements to work its magic – *capital growth*, which is determined by the rate of interest you receive; and *time*, or how long you receive that interest and allow it to multiply. Time is the most important element in this equation, which is what most people lose when they tell themselves that 'now is not a good time to start saving, I'll just wait until…' and fill in the blank from your own life. We'll look at this factor first, and then explore capital growth.

Let's use the example of 18-year-old twins, Grace and Peter. They look identical, but they have very different attitudes to money. Grace, the wise human ant, immediately begins to save $1,000 a year into a safe interest-bearing account until she reaches the age of 30, at which point she stops contributing to her savings account and instead puts the same amount toward purchasing a home. Of course, we recommend that nothing stop you from making regular savings, but for the sake of this example we'll just say that she at least doesn't touch her 13 years' worth of savings and allows them to accumulate.

Peter, on the other hand, has lived 'the good life' like a happy little grasshopper and not saved anything, but when he sees Grace not only having savings but now a home, he gets a little worried and decides he'd better do something. At age 30 he begins to save not $1,000 but *$2,000* a year into the same account that Grace used, thinking he'll not only catch up but soon pass her, and for ease of calculation we'll again say that both receive 10% interest on their savings. One saves for 13 years and the other for 35 years, so who do you think will be wealthiest at age 65, and by how much?

Having invested $70,000 (35 years X $2,000), with interest Peter will have $542,000 – which is not bad. But Grace, having invested a total of only $13,000 (13 years X $1,000), will have an incredible *$690,000*. How is this possible? It doesn't seem to make sense, but thanks to the power of compounding over time, Grace's savings at age 30 ($24,500) were already giving her an annual return of $2,450 ($450 more than her brother's contribution), and it continued to exceed his by an increasing margin every single year. This is possible only because *time* was on Grace's side, a crucial element to compounding your savings and investments.

We know it's hard to believe, so read it over again or do the calculations yourself until you're sure. And in the meantime, here's another story from George Clayson's 'The Richest Man In Babylon' to help you get even clearer on the importance of disciplined saving, and the power of compounding. In this extract, the would-be rich man is boasting of his success to his mentor, Algamish.

"I have paid myself faithfully," I replied, "and my savings I have entrusted to Agger the shield maker, to buy bronze, and each fourth month he does pay me the rental."

"That is good. And what do you do with the rental?" asked Algamish.

"I do have a great feast with honey and fine wine and spiced cake. Also, I have bought me a scarlet tunic. And some day, I shall buy me a young ass upon which to ride."

To which Algamish laughed; "You do eat the children of your savings. Then how do you expect them to work for you? And how can they have children that will also work for you? First get thee an army of golden slaves, and then many a rich banquet may you enjoy without regret."

Many people begin saving, say $3000-$4000 a year, and at the end of three of four years have 'only' $12,000, so they abandon their plan and discipline, and spend it. Financially, they're like a dieter in reverse who loses weight, then binges and gains it all back and more – they gain money, then lose it all and more. The power of compounding only reveals itself with time, and not only increases but *accelerates*.

Remember the wisdom of Algamish the next time you're tempted to delay or skimp or rob your hard-earned immortality account, to 'eat the children of your savings', and one day you too will have a golden army to do your bidding. Again, earning the right to rule that army takes discipline, to not take the easy way (which in the long term is actually anything but easy), and do what most people are not willing to do. It's illogical to think that you can act like one of the many, yet become one of the few.

> ## *'I find television very educational.*
> ## *Every time somebody turns it on*
> ## *I go into another room and read a book.'*
> ~ Groucho Marx ~

Clear enough? Are you convinced? Okay, now let's look at the second element of compounding – capital growth, also knows as the *rate of return*. You want to get the highest interest rate possible for your money, for as long as possible, and here is another excellent reason to start early and save regularly, with the best interest you can find. There's an old economic rule called 'The Law of 72' which shows how long it takes for your money to double in value.

To work it out, simply divide the interest rate into 72. No one seems to be quite sure why this simple formula works, but it does, and it certainly makes things a lot clearer. So if you were to have $100,000 in a fixed term account (which you will do if you stick to the plan) at the easily computed 10% interest rate, let's see what happens. Divide 72 by 10 and you know that in 7.2 years, without making any further deposits and disregarding bank fees and capital gains tax, your $100,000 will double to $200,000. In 14.4 years it will grow to $400,000; and after less than 30 years your $100,000 will have become $800,000! Not bad for a passive investment that requires nothing but the original amount and your signature, is it? This illustrates what we meant when we spoke of having money work for you, about being its master rather than its slave, and being free to do what you'd love rather than what you have to do.

If you were to receive not 10% but 7%, it would take your money 72 / 7 = 10.3 years to double. The difference of just 3% compounded over time means that your investment at 7% would grow to $196,715 in 10 years as opposed to $259,374 at 10%. The difference of $62,659 is what you would have made, or lost, depending on your rate of return. So don't discount the tremendous importance of time, and seemingly small numbers that very quickly grow to become big numbers. Imagine the combined effects of your continual deposits over decades with this rate of doubling occurring simultaneously in 3 to 7 levels of savings and investment, and you can see how real wealth is possible for anyone, including you, and the sooner you start the more certain it will be.

At its heart, compounding is simple arithmetic – it uses the multiplication of dollars and time to increase your wealth. But there is one more level of compounding that we wish to share with you, even though it's too soon for you to start making use of it immediately. However, when the time comes you'll at least be informed enough to understand the principle and take even further advantage of the laws of financial mastery. That final stage is called 'leveraging', and it relies on using your existing assets to borrow more and increase your returns.

Leverage, or 'gearing' as it is commonly called, is nothing more than the process of borrowing money for the purpose of investment. By adding those borrowed funds to your own, you increase the amount available for investment and get much greater advantage from the multiplication of time and capital growth. The returns, as a proportion of your original capital, are 'geared up' or magnified. The rich, who simply started on this path to wealth creation sooner than you did and learned its lessons in exactly the same way, have long known that by borrowing money and investing it wisely they can create far more than if they had relied on their own capital alone. We're going to use some equations that may seem a bit obscure at first, but we'll do our best to keep it simple, and with just a little patience (the topic of our next chapter), it will come clear for you.

The principle of leverage comes from engineering, where a little force moves a heavy weight through the use of a lever, and in the same way financial leverage can be described as using a small amount of cash to move a much larger one. The power of leverage is shown in the equation:

Load (100 kg)/Effort (10 kg) = Leverage (10 to 1)

So using a lever in this example, it only takes 10 kilos of effort to lift 100 kilos of load. The load of 100 kilos divided by an effort of 10 kilos yields a leverage of 10 to 1 (10:1). If you tried to simply lift a weight of 100 kilos with your arms, you'd have to use 100 kilos of effort, which means that the leverage is 1:1 – one kilo of effort yields one kilo of lift, which is no leverage at all.

The same principle applies to finance, and all you do is change the terms. Here the *load* is the value of the assets you've gained by borrowing, the *effort* is your financial contribution or what they cost you, and the *leverage* is your profit or rate of return. The formula then becomes:

Asset Value ($)/Your Commitment ($) = Financial Leverage

Now let's put you into the equation and see what it looks like in real life. If you had an extra $60 a week you could choose to do one of three things with it:

1. *Spend* it (and by now we hope your automatic response is 'No way!').
2. *Save* it into an interest-bearing account.

3. *Leverage* it, ie use the $60 to service the loan on an investment port-
folio (property or shares) worth $100,000.

Having rejected the poverty strategy of the first option, for the sake
of simplicity we'll say the other two both give you a return of 10%, and
we'll set aside the effects of bank charges, borrowing costs, and taxes.
At the end of the year you'll have invested a total of $3,120 ($60 X 52
weeks), but the two options have very different outcomes.

The savings account, option 2, will give you $312 (10% of $3,120). If
you instead choose option 3, to leverage your $60 and use it to borrow
$100,000 and invest in property or shares, the cost of the loan would be
met by your returns (either rent or dividends), and your $60 per week
would make up any shortfall between your cost and profit. At the end of
the year you've still made your 10%, but the question is, 10% of what? In
this case, it's not just your contribution of $3,120 but the entire borrowed
amount, and 10% of $100,000 is $10,000. For the same investment, the
returns are either $312 or $10,000, and *that* is the power of leveraging.
Then, of course, compounding takes effect and the difference becomes
even greater with each passing year.

> **'Give me a lever long enough and a place to stand,**
> **and I will move the world.'**
> ~ Archimedes ~

To make sure you understand, let's do it again to give you a more
detailed picture of how it works. We'll up the ante this time, and assume
you have $100,000 in the bank. Now that you're too smart to spend it,
you have two options:

1. Invest $100,000 in a portfolio of managed funds that you would
   own outright.
2. Use the $100,000 to borrow (or leverage) $500,000 and use that to
   buy half a million dollars worth of the same managed funds or
   property.

Put the numbers of the first option into our formula to determine the
leverage, and you get:

Asset Value ($)/Your Commitment ($) = Financial Leverage
$100,000/$100,000 = 1:1

So this option has a gearing ratio of 1:1 – which is a leverage factor of 1 (that is, *no* leverage).

The second option is a little different, and it looks like this:

$500,000/$100,000 = 5:1

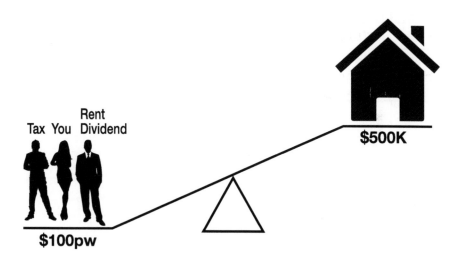

The gearing ratio is 5:1, so the leverage is 5, which is really quite a small number. But let's see what happens when we run that number out over ten years, again using an interest rate of 10%, knowing that while the actual numbers may be less, the proportions will be the same.

Years	Option 1		Option 2	
	Value	Growth	Value	Growth
1	$100,000	$10,000	$500,000	$50,000
2	$110,000	$11,000	$550,000	$55,000
3	$121,000	$12,100	$605,000	$60,500
4	$133,100	$13,310	$665,500	$66,550
5	$146,410	$14,641	$732,050	$73,205
6	$161,051	$16,105	$805,255	$80,526
7	$177,156	$17,716	$885,781	$88,578
8	$194,872	$19,487	$974,359	$97,436
9	$214,359	$21,436	$1,071,794	$107,179
10	$235,795	$23,579	$1,178,974	$117,897
	Total	$159,374	Total	$796,871

You can see that it's much easier to accumulate $1,000,000 worth of growth assets through leveraging than it is to save $1,000,000 – it's the ancient principle of using 'Other People's Money' to increase your own. Through borrowed funds you combine your assets with the wealth of a bank or building society, giving you access to a much greater portfolio of assets than you could manage on your own.

Familiarity makes new concepts clearer, so we'll use an image that everyone knows. The pedals (that's you) on a bicycle have a small rotation, but gears (the bank) magnify the rotation of the wheels and move you forward much faster. In the same way leveraging, *if used properly*, can help build your wealth more quickly, yielding greater financial advantage with a smaller amount of effort. Use bigger gears and your bicycle moves faster, use gearing and your wealth grows faster.

Once again, it's obvious how powerful the combination of dollars, time, and compounding can be, and how you can use them to create real and lasting wealth for yourself. Of course there are risks associated, and variables such as your income and ability to service your debt, interest rates, stock and property market fluctuations, housing availability, and national and international economies, all make this a much more complex affair. Leveraging should not be undertaken without a stable financial foundation, a lot of personal experience, and skilled professional advice, but at least you now know what it is and will be better prepared to use it in the future. It's yet another motivation and reward for having the discipline to save *now*.

Far too many investors have been seduced by the potential for great wealth through leveraging, over-extended themselves, and then were brought crashing down by an unexpected development in one or more of these many variables. In terms of the Investment Pyramid, leveraging should not come into your dealings until level 5 or 6; by then you should have enough financial knowledge and experience to attempt it with relative safety, and when the time comes you can maximise your benefits and minimise the potential risks by following these guidelines:

Gear Conservatively

Don't overextend your borrowings. Carefully consider your ability to meet interest payments and possible interest rate changes, bank crises, taxes, fluctuating property values, and rental returns.

Diversify Your Investment Portfolio

Never rely exclusively on one investment, or one type of investment. Even if it's your favourite basket, it's unwise to put all your eggs into it.

Invest For The Long Term

To ride out the inevitable and unpredictable fluctuations of the share market, invest for a minimum of five years, and preferably seven or more.

Have A Reasonable Cash Flow

A stable, regular income is essential to meet your interest expenses – don't rely solely on dividend income to make your contribution.

Build In Flexibility

Do not be forced into a position where you might have to sell when you don't choose to. Build in flexibility, diversity, and financial buffers to cope with any unexpected personal, employment, or market changes. Yet again, savings will help you here.

Seek Professional Advice

Gearing can be extremely effective, if done correctly, so always consult with experts (more than one) in this field to create a plan that suits you personally.

Speak to qualified professionals to get the benefits of their knowledge and experience in the details, but the decision to set it all in train and make this golden future a present reality lies with you – it all starts with the *saving*. There really is no such thing as a free lunch, but courage and intelligence are assets that both human beings and the universe itself honour and reward.

So there you have it – a 3-chapter outline of all the practical steps you need to know in order to become wealthy. If it seems too easy, great! That means you can relax, knowing it's possible for you. If it seems too easy to be true – try it and see.

Have you ever begun something that you thought was beyond you, or even impossible, and then found strength and help along the way that made it all possible? Have the will and wisdom to act in your own best interests, and the interests of your loved ones (because they will learn from your example), and you'll receive unexpected assistance from the physical, the mathematical, and even the metaphysical worlds.

In the third and final part of this book we're going to bring it all together – the 'being' of Part One and the 'doing' of Part Two will become a new element in Part Three – 'having'.

'When one is willing and eager,
the gods join in.'
~ Aeschylus ~

~ EXERCISE ~

1. The opportunities in this chapter will come to you naturally as a result of following all our previous instructions, we just wanted you to have even more motivation to begin and commit to your savings. However, the old saying, 'I hear and I forget, I see and I remember, I do and I understand,' has real truth, so we'd like you to experience the reality of this remarkable phenomenon of compounding. You won't need a chessboard and an ocean of rice, a calculator will do very nicely.

Start with the number 1, multiply it by 2, then multiply that result by 2 again, and keep repeating the doubling 64 times (the number of squares on a chessboard). The number will eventually grow so large your calculator's screen won't be able to display it and you'll have to resort to pen and paper, but stay with it and the results will astonish you. Careful, long-term investment lies at the heart of all the world's great fortunes.

2. We'd also like you to experience the power of money to reproduce, to magnetically attract more of itself, so this chapter has a second exercise. Decide how much money you'd love to earn in a day, and begin carrying that amount in a separate section of your wallet or purse. This money is not for spending, although it's there if you need it; it has a more subtle, dual purpose. One, it will change your consciousness about larger sums of money, and by familiarity you'll come to see that amount as normal and feel you deserve to have it – that's the inner effect. Two, the outer effect, is that money is magnetic, and carrying it automatically attracts more into your life.

Some people say they'd be afraid to lose it, but if you fear to lose something you also fear to gain it, and by now you know that emotion sabotages wealth. Besides, it *works* – your income will increase to match the amount you carry with you, and losing one day's income is no great hardship. The combination of physical and metaphysical power in this exercise is profound, and is also a very simple way to transform your relationship with wealth.

'A great pleasure in life is doing what people say you cannot do.'
~ Walter Gagehot ~

PART THREE
INNER AND OUTER WEALTH
~ HAVING ~

Chapter 7

The Power of Patience
All Things Come to Those Who Wait

*'The stock market is a financial redistribution system.
It takes money away from those who have no patience
and gives it to those who have.'*
~ Warren Buffet ~

Congratulations, you've come a long way along the path to financial freedom, success, and even more importantly – wisdom. In the previous three chapters we set out all the fiscal knowledge and information you need to make your way in the world of wealth creation. It will take time and experience to truly absorb them until they're as natural and familiar to you as the rest of your life already is, but if you stay focused and disciplined, it's inevitable. As you may recall, our first three chapters were not about outer wealth at all, but about inner self-worth and power. We'll now bring together the inner *being* and the outer *doing*, without which no lasting fortune is possible – *being* plus *doing* equals *having*.

In these last two chapters, we're going back inside to address the state of mind and spirit that are so vital for success in this world. So far we've been asking you to use your intellect, but from here on there will be nothing to memorise, no discipline to apply – the hard work is over and all you need to do now is listen with your heart. Allow the stories and philosophy to strengthen the part of you that is naturally unique and gifted and inspired, that is delighted to be here with all the opportunities that surround us, and to have been given the precious gift of life. And just as we're going to bring the inner qualities and outer abilities together, so too do the final financial laws and universal principles now merge into one Truth.

A quality question to ask at this point is; Why do the vast majority of people fail to accumulate wealth? The same answer comes from many sources: popular wisdom says we always seek the easiest way to get the things we want, and usually we want them *right now*; economists believe that the inability to delay gratification is a primary contributor to failure later in life; and the famous salesman and motivator Brian Tracy called it the 'Expediency Factor' or 'E Factor' – the inability to form and follow long-term plans. The words are similar, and the effects are the same the world over.

A young man drops out of school to earn money so he can buy a car to impress girls – the hidden cost is a probable life of low wages and unfulfilling jobs. Rather than take the time to prepare a nutritious meal, people in ever-increasing numbers turn to fast food, accurately called 'junk food' – the result is obesity, blocked arteries, reduced vitality, and a shortened life. Criminals rob and steal to get money quickly – and risk wasting their lives in prison. Most people find a 'steady' job and do the minimum to receive their pay, then spend the rest of their time socialising, watching television, and sleeping – not realising that the price is a life without greatness or wealth. Each of these life choices is motivated by an irresistible desire for immediate gratification, to get pleasure or happiness or riches quickly, and every one of them trades small short-term gain for great long-term pain.

It's painful to see this in your parents, and you wouldn't wish it on your children, so why should you let it happen to you? Fortunately, you now have the choice to create a different future, and our sixth Truth is a huge factor in that decision:

Financial & Universal Truth ~6 ~
Patience, Patience, Patience

Nothing worthwhile happens overnight. There is a natural rhythm to all aspects of life, and it takes time to grow a flower or a tree, to plant a garden or build a house, to create a work of art, for a child to become an adult, or for a fortune to be made. Even writing this book took time and research and effort, not to mention the decades of learning and experience that made it possible, and when you truly care about something you'll take the time to make it the best it can be.

'The tastiest ice cream is the hardest to scoop.'
~ Apu Nahasapenapetalan ~

When we allow our impatience to rule us and try to force events into unnatural haste, there is always a price to pay. Pulling at a little green shoot kills the plant that would otherwise have grown tall. Dig shallow foundations, and the building will not stand. Those who attempt to get rich quickly very rarely make it, and of the few who do even fewer keep their wealth, because they didn't learn how to master it on the way. There is an old Zen story used to teach this principle to new students.

Long ago, in medieval Japan, a man heard of the power of enlightenment and its ability to lift those who attained it beyond the trials of this world. He became quite excited, and the very next morning he rose before dawn and went to the local Zen monastery. He knocked long and hard until a monk finally opened the gate and asked him what he wanted.

The man said, "I want to become enlightened. How long does it take?"

The monk scratched his shaven head and replied, "About 20 years, usually."

The man was dismayed to hear this and asked, "What if I work extra hard? How long then?"

The monk thought a moment before answering, "Probably 30 years."

The man spluttered, "No, you don't understand. What if I get up early every morning and stay up late every night, and work harder at it than anyone ever has before? How long will it take me to become enlightened then?"

The monk squinted up at the sky and said, "Oh, in that case – 40 years."
The man was outraged, thinking he was being mocked; "That makes
no sense! How can working harder take more time?" and the monk
smiled at him; "When someone is as impatient as you, everything takes
much longer."

The body's fastest-growing cells are actually cancerous, and the
fastest-growing examples in the history of finance are the railway shares
craze of the early 19th century, the U.S. stock market before the crash of
1929, the dotcom bubble of 2000, and the phenomenal returns from the
bogus investments of Bernie Madoff, the stockbroker who in 2008 was
found to have 'made off' with an estimated $65 to $85 billion in a fraud
spanning over 35 years, and is now spending 150 years in prison (release
date November 14, 2139) for his world-record thefts. They all sounded
wonderful at the time, the masses jumped on board for fear of being left
behind, and they all ended up swallowing vast amounts of money and
teaching people what *not* to do. The form keeps changing, which is why
every generation gets fooled again, but the lesson remains the same – if it
sounds too good to be true, it probably is.

Gold flees the man who would force it to impossible earnings, or who
followeth the alluring advice of tricksters and schemers, or who trusts
it to his own experience and romantic desires in investment. Fanciful
propositions that thrill like adventure tales always come to the new
owner of gold. These appear to endow his treasure with magic powers
that will enable it to make impossible earnings. Yet heed ye the wise men,
for verily they know the risks that lurk behind every plan to make great
wealth suddenly.
~ George Clayson ~ 'The Richest Man in Babylon'

It's been true throughout history, and it's true now – impatience
sabotages and delays wealth. So if you really want to create a stable
and lasting fortune, relax! We don't suggest you fall asleep, but neither
should you froth at the mouth. In its first year of business Coca-cola
sold the grand total of 400 bottles of soft drink – about one bottle a day.

Without patience, it would not have grown to the multi-billion dollar company it is today. The system we've laid out for you works, it has stood the test of time, and the faster you try to push things and the greedier you become, the more money you'll lose, the more painful lessons you'll repeat, and the longer it will take. Have patience, stay with your plan, follow the example and advice of those who have gone before you, and grow slowly but surely.

> **'The haste of a fool is the slowest thing in the world.'**
> ~ Thomas Shadwell ~

Realism, not fantasy, is where true success and wealth lie, and speaking of realism, let's be honest about where you are right now. If you were able to buy this book, if you have a house or flat with electricity and running water, if you have a bank account, a phone, a refrigerator with food in it, and you eat every day, you are already wealthier than 90% of the 7 billion people on this planet. That doesn't mean you shouldn't seek more, but you'd be wise to appreciate what you already have.

Tim ~ part III

A client came to see me about 10 years ago. I'd previously helped him resolve some challenges in his marriage, and now he had another problem. He sat down, I asked him how I could be of service, and he blurted out, "I want more money! I'm sick and tired of working my guts out and just making enough to get by. I want a bigger house and holidays every year and a new car and a motorcycle, and I don't want to be looked down on by everyone who has more than I do!"

I asked him, "Okay, so where are you already wealthy? What form is it in?" and he snapped, "Don't give me that philosophy crap! I just want money, a lot of it, and I want it now, and if you can't help me I'll find someone who can. For some reason I'm so angry about this I can hardly sleep."

He was a chef, so I said, "Say you invited me to your restaurant for a beautiful meal that you had specially prepared, and after dessert I just walked out without a word. Would you invite me again?"

"Ha! If you were so ungrateful I wouldn't even let you back in, let alone give you more. But what's that got to do with anything?"

"Don't you realise that the universe is exactly the same? We're built on the same principles, and if you're not grateful for what you've already been given, why would it want to give you more?"

That stopped him for a moment, and he said, "I guess that's so, I never though of it that way. But I still want and need more money!"

"So who are you already richer than?"

"What?"

"Are you better off than most of the people in Africa?"

"Well, of course I am, those people are starving to death."

"Are you wealthier than most people in Central and South America?"

"Uh, yeah – there's terrible poverty there."

"Are you wealthier than most people in India and China?"

"Absolutely!"

"Well, there are over 2 billion people in those two countries alone, and I guarantee you're also wealthier than most people in the Middle East, and Southeast Asia, and Eastern Europe, and Russia, the Pacific Islands and the Caribbean... In fact, you're probably already in the top 5% of wealth in the world, and yet you're complaining and angry and ungrateful. If you're not thankful for what you have, why would the universe give you more?"

This time it got in, and he suddenly realised how fortunate he was, how much he'd been taking for granted, and how much he had to be grateful for. He'd been focusing on the few who had more than he did, and forgetting the vast majority who had so much less. That man was humbled, suddenly stopped complaining about his life, and he left my office in an entirely different frame of mind. He called me about a month later to say he'd been offered another job as head chef in a new restaurant, with a big pay increase.

He was very puzzled; "I don't understand it. I didn't do anything different, and suddenly all this money shows up."

I said, "Yes, you did. You got grateful."

Do not underestimate the power of sincere, heartfelt gratitude to transform your circumstances and your life.

'The foolish curse roses for having thorns.
The wise are grateful that thorns have roses.'

If you're smart, you'll find and appreciate how successful you already are. It's very difficult to go from being a failure to a success, but much easier to go from being a success in one level or area to even greater success in another. A 2011 report by the World Health Organisation stated that an Australian on the dole is in the top 6% of wealth in the world. This ancient saying also applies to gratitude; 'To those who have (gratitude), more is given. To those who have not, more is taken away', until they wake up and give thanks for what they've already received.

Gratitude and patience are extremely powerful forces. And please don't misunderstand the nature of patience – it is not a passive or weak state at all; in fact, real patience requires unusual strength. We all have it, but few of us ever call upon it. This story may help you to face your own challenges, when they come; it's what we mean by the strength of patience.

There was a man born into extreme poverty, whose father used him as nothing but a serf or workhorse until he left home at the age of 21. He never saw or spoke to his father again, but set himself up in a little business, and failed that same year. He ran for the state legislature at 22 and was defeated, then went bankrupt again at 24. At 26 he was devastated when the girl he loved died, and at 27 he suffered a nervous breakdown. At 34 he ran for congress and lost, and lost again 2 years later. He tried to become a senator at 45 and lost, attempted to win the vice-presidential nomination 2 years later and – yes, he lost. He went on to lose another senatorial race 2 years after that, and at the age of 52 he... became the 16th, and many believe the greatest, president of the United States of America. That man was Abraham Lincoln.

Any one of those countless setbacks could have crushed his spirit, and most people would have given up, or at least stopped trying, which is the sneaky way of giving up. But instead of defeating him, every challenge and tragedy only made him stronger. Because he refused to surrender, he triumphed, and the same principle applies to all of us – if you don't give up, you cannot lose. He learned from everything that happened to him, didn't become disheartened or bitter, and even joked about his many defeats; "Well, I feel just like the boy who stubbed his toe – too damned badly hurt to laugh, and too damned proud to cry."

'It's impossible to live a life without failing,
unless you live a life so small it was hardly worth living.'
~ J.K. Rowling ~

And strangely enough, for many people the real danger lies not in defeat or failure, but in success. Sometimes, those who met every challenge and faced every adversity go all to pieces when things start going their way. Why? Forewarned is forearmed, so let's hear what happened to John after he achieved his great goal of becoming rich.

John's Story ~ Conclusion

More than anything else, I dreamed of being a millionaire, and that dream sustained me through all the setbacks and challenges I had to face along the way. I focused on it to the exclusion of everything else, and simply couldn't see any other outcome – I was going to make it no matter what! I put together a team of good people who were not only highly skilled, they cared about me and always covered my back. I had ambition and people skills (sometimes called charisma) to burn, but the truth is that I was never very good on detail; I lacked the patience for it, so I was fortunate that my staff were always there to make up for the areas I was weak in.

We started out selling investment properties from a tiny office on the first floor of a building in Parramatta. As time passed we grew, slowly at first and then ever faster, until eventually we took over the entire first floor and half the third, and our one company became four. The property company needed to advertise, so I set up a marketing wing. People needed financing to purchase properties, so rather than give away that business the obvious next step was to open my own finance company. As my clients made money and their income tax returns became more complex, I saw another opportunity and started my own accounting firm. At one point I employed 40 finance brokers, becoming the largest Australian introducer of business to Citi Bank. And the money rolled in.

I had everything I ever dreamed of; a beautiful home, a loving wife and two children, a Porsche 911 and a V12 750 BMW, and more money than I could spend (and God knows I spent a lot!). Every month I'd have two stretch limousines out front to take my two top producers from each company and my senior managers out to celebrate our success. I'd buy each winner a new suit and complete outfit at a quality haberdasher, and then off we'd go to a different top restaurant where the champagne would flow and lunch might last 'til 11 at night.

I was wealthy, successful, respected… and ashamed. I had a vision of my own future, and apart from wealth it included computer skills, the ability to write a comprehensive business plan, a knowledge of law, an understanding of balance sheets, marketing, strategy, and mastery of all the countless details necessary to run a successful business. But the companies had such momentum, and the money came so fast, that I never had time to develop all these arcane skills, and the bigger we grew the worse I felt. In meetings with lawyers and accountants I would nod wisely as they gave me their incomprehensible advice; after all, I was 'the boss' and made more money than all of them put together. But inside I was humiliated and afraid that someone would find out who I really was, and it would all come crashing down around me. My god, I was so dyslexic that even reading reports was a challenge to me! What right did a 'wog boy' from a poor family in a housing commission have to all of this? I was making money for everyone – my clients and employees, the banks and developers, the tax department, but inside I felt a complete fraud.

*I was too young to understand that there are no errors in this world, that there is a universal balance behind all things, and my wealth came to me for good reason. I'm far enough away in time now to see that young man more clearly, and appreciate his qualities without taking them personally; the power of my vision and certainty, my enthusiasm, honesty, and innocence, my genuine caring for people and desire to help them improve the quality of their lives, the 'charisma' that brought all these experts together in a way they couldn't manage for themselves, and most of all because I simply wanted it more than anybody I ever met. But I didn't see that, all I saw was what I **didn't** have. I didn't feel worthy of my success, and just as with a lottery winner, whatever we don't feel we deserve is taken away.*

The beginning of the end came when my chief accountant walked into my office one day and said, "John, we're ready to go international. I've set up a meeting with a top American firm, and their directors are flying out to set things up next month. This is the big time, baby!"

That was it for me. I was already hiding from Australia, and now I'd have to hide from America as well? That weekend I went from the high life to the low life, started doing things that only the biggest losers in society turn to, and by the time the meeting came around the Americans recognised the signs. They told my accountant they liked the hell out of me, as most people still did, but they wouldn't work with me. From that point on I stopped doing the things that took me to the top – visualising goals, inspiring others, being disciplined – which I've since learned is very common when success comes too fast or too big for the understanding of the poor bugger who makes it. My companies were so successful, and my people were so loyal and good, that it took several years to throw it all away, but in the end I managed it. I lost the companies, the money, my house and cars, my wife and children, my friends, my self-respect, my health, and very nearly my life.

*Eventually I hit bottom and, against all the odds, started to come back up again. I'm rising now, what they call 'a sadder and a wiser man', and you better believe I appreciate every day and dollar that God sends me. Now when I teach, I know the whole story – not just how to make money, but how to **keep** it, so the time was not wasted and others can benefit from my folly. So what's the moral of the story? Don't be too impatient for wealth, appreciate the journey, be grateful and thankful for whatever you receive, and finally… If a poor, under-educated, dyslexic wog like me can become a millionaire, anybody can do it, including you.*

'One who is skilled in defeat shall never see destruction.'
~ Tai Gong Wong ~

John and Abraham Lincoln aren't alone in finding the climb to the top much harder and longer than they expected it to be. A weed can spring up overnight, but it takes time for a great oak to reach its full growth and beauty. You must decide which you want to be, a weed or a tree; but without persevering patience, you won't even have the choice.

If you read the lives of any great man or woman throughout history, their success came after years of challenge and difficulty. As for those who didn't find the will to stay true... well, they lived their lives, but we don't know how because no one remembers them. Here are some stories of people that everyone knows, with good reason.

Nelson Mandela was a poor African with a vision of equality for his entire nation and continent. Because he dared to stand up against the powers of his day and say, "No, there is a better way," they made an example of him and sent him to prison for 27 years. It would have been easy to become angry and bitter, or to surrender to despair, and 999 people out of 1000 would have done exactly that, but he was the thousandth. Instead of becoming angry, he studied and expanded his understanding; instead of despairing, he thought deeply and expanded his spirit. His guards later said that unlike the other prisoners he never resented them, but always had a kind word and a calm demeanour throughout nearly three decades locked in a room 8 feet wide and 10 feet long.

Upon his release he was elected the first black president of his country, travelled the world speaking with the heads of nations, became a living symbol of freedom and the power of patient certainty, and his speeches are famous for their wisdom and nobility. One of our wives had the honour to meet him when he visited Sydney, and she said, "I've met a lot of people with presence, but he had *Presence*. It was like a field that surrounded him for about 15 feet; as you approached time seemed to slow down, and all you could see was him."

We visited an art gallery in the Rocks area of Sydney a few years ago, and on an easel in the entranceway was a large white sheet of paper, in a frame and under glass, with a handprint in the centre. The girl at the desk said Mr Mandela had made it as a poster for one of his many charities. She then told us to look closely, and we saw that in the centre of the palm, where his hand was slightly raised and no ink had touched him, was an almost perfect map of Africa. The sticker read 'Print 947 of 1000', and the price was $20,000. We multiplied $20,000 by 1000 and realised that simply by dipping his hand in ink, taking perhaps 20 seconds, he had generated $20,000,000. That's $20 million a second! How many people in the world, after a lifetime of hard work, could match it? Don't believe that patience is not rewarded.

'All things are difficult before they are easy.'
~ John Morley ~

Pierre Elliot Trudeau was the most internationally renowned, flamboyant, charismatic Prime Minister Canada ever had. He was a good friend of then-U.S. president Jimmy Carter, a country boy uncomfortable with international diplomacy. Jimmy asked him to come down and help whenever he was forced to host conferences with other world leaders, and Pierre's sophistication and language skills always smoothed the way for the Georgia farmer. Elected an unprecedented four times, Trudeau did more than any Prime Minister before or since to unite the French- and English-speaking factions of his nation, established independence from Great Britain, and forged the Canadian constitution. Yet at the age of 40 he was still living at home with his mother, and had never held a paying job in his life – his time simply hadn't come yet, but when it did he was ready.

In 2008, through a series of market fluctuations and unwise business decisions, Australian businessman **James Packer** was losing $8,000 a minute, $480,000 an hour, or $11.5 million a day, every single day, day after day after day. He lost a total of $4 billion that year, and yet he didn't let the jeering criticism of others (and there was plenty) or his own fears stop him. He knew it was the nature of business and life to rise and fall, and because he persevered, he's back on top and regrowing his vast fortune.

'Only the mediocre are always at their best.'
~ Jean Giraudoux ~

In 1939, **Judy Garland** was paid $35 a week for filming 'The Wizard of Oz' – her little dog Toto (real name Terry) made $125. Although the studio didn't respect her, she respected herself, and who's immortal now? Despite decades of career setbacks, broken marriages, and alcohol and drug use, she never stopped singing because she loved it, and became one of the most successful and famous performers in the world. Her daughter, Liza Minelli, told this story about her mother: In the 1950s, a gushing fan approached her in the ladies room of a nightclub where she was performing and said, "Judy, how did you manage to survive so much heartbreak?" and as she swept out of the room Judy tossed back over her shoulder; "Because I've got rainbows up my ass!" She had spirit and never gave up, which is why she's still world-famous today.

'What is to give light must endure burning.'
~ Viktor Frankl ~

After the tremendous success of 'Monty Python's Flying Circus', comedian **John Cleese** became annoyed at the poor quality of situation comedies on television. When challenged to do better he said, "All right, I will, just to prove that it's possible." He wrote several scripts for his new show, sent them in to the BBC, and still has framed on his office wall the one-line report by the executive who rejected the whole project. It reads *'I can't see this being anything other than a disaster.'* The program was 'Fawlty Towers' – now honoured as a classic. He had to write it, fight the BBC bureaucracy to get it approved, play the lead role, and direct the episodes, but because he believed in it, millions around the world are still laughing – not *at* him, but *with* him.

An English band in the 70s had been playing together for years without success, and in desperation they pooled everything they had to go to America for one last grab at the golden ring. They played a series of increasingly shabby venues, running out of opportunities and money and hope, until one night they found themselves playing a seedy little New York bar called 'The Last Chance Saloon'. There were only five people in the audience, but rather than coast through the set they gathered them all together at one table in front, introduced themselves, and proceeded to play every song they knew, as hard and loud and well as they could, to the applause of their surprised audience.

After three encores they joined their 'fans' at the table for drinks, and one of them said, "That was a great gig! I'm a DJ on a local radio station, do you guys have a tape of your music?" They did, he played it on air, it went national, and everything changed. The band's name was **'The Police'**.

Colonel Sanders was a 65 year-old retiree living on a pension in the Deep South when he went into a diner one day and ordered a roast chicken dinner. The quality was so poor that he couldn't stop thinking about it. He knew he could do better, so when he got home he searched out an old recipe of his mother's, and went back to the diner offering to cook their chicken for them. He didn't want any money, just a chance to find out if the recipe was a good as he thought it was and see how the public responded to it, but even as a free service they weren't interested. Surprised and disappointed, he went to another café and made them the same offer, with exactly the same results – they weren't going to let any old coot in their kitchen no matter how good his chicken was.

Now he wasn't disappointed, he was irritated, and he had an idea. With no job and nothing but time on his hands, he got in his car and started to drive through the South, sampling the chicken wherever he went and offering to help them do it better if they'd just give him a chance. With refusal after refusal it became a mission, and he kept records of all the places he visited. In the end he went to *1,006* restaurants, cafes, diners and roadhouses before he found one willing even to give him a chance, and the rest really is history.

A good idea is the start, but it takes perseverance and determination to achieve success, and Colonel Sanders' refusal to take 'no' for an answer led to the creation of a multi-billion dollar, international business chain. The average child falls down 8,000 times before they learn to walk. 8,000 times! There is something inside us all that will not be denied, no matter how many apparent 'failures' there are along the way. There's no such thing as failure, it's all just practice, and practice makes perfect – every 'no' you experience on the way is just refining you towards the 'yes'. How big is your dream? How many times are you prepared to fall and not let it stop you?

'Fall seven times, stand up eight.'
~ Samurai proverb ~

Early in the 20th century a young **Walt Disney** worked as an illustrator for an eastern newspaper, but his dream was to go to Hollywood and become an animator in the movie industry. So one day he gathered his courage, quit his job, and took his tiny savings off to California to seek his fortune. He knew he was good, so it would only be a matter of time before he landed a plum job at one of the big studios for a great salary, possibly as much as $25 or even $50 a week!

But when he arrived on the coast things didn't go quite as planned; it was hard to get an interview at the studios – they just weren't interested in a young, unknown illustrator, and competition was much fiercer than he expected. It seemed everyone was unemployed and willing to work for peanuts, and his money was running out fast. He went from decent hotel to shabby hotel to boarding house, until he had no money left and no idea what to do. He couldn't go back home a failure, but he couldn't afford to stay where he was, and there seemed no way out.

One day in desperation he went into a church and prayed for help, then just sat there in the pew because he had nowhere else to go. The minister noticed the young man sitting so dejectedly with his bags at his side, and spoke to him. Walt had been alone so long that he found himself pouring out his troubles to a sympathetic ear, and when he finished the minister said, "Maybe things aren't quite as hopeless as you imagine. Come with me, young man." He drove Walt to his own house nearby, then took him around the back and down some stairs to the basement. He said, "It's not much, and quite frankly no one else would live here, but this will be your home for as long as you need it."

Walt was moved by his generosity and thanked the man profusely, but when he was alone again he looked around and his heart sank. The place was low-ceilinged and filthy, full of rubbish and cobwebs and old broken furniture, with no electricity, and the floor was just dirt. He thought to himself, *I have no money, no job, no home, and no prospects. I don't think I can go any lower than this*, and for a while he despaired. But he was young, and soon he got up and began cleaning the place. Among the trash he found an old desk that he could work on, so during the day he would look for a job and at night he would spend hours drawing, perfecting his talent for the opportunity he hoped would come.

To make matters worse, he found that the place was infested with mice, and as he worked at night by lantern light they would scurry all over the floor. But he was lonely, so he would sometimes feed them crumbs from his dinner, and he became particularly attached to one mouse that would sit on the desk and take food from his hand.

He named that mouse Mortimer, began to draw him, and from those drawings came Steamboat Willie, and Mickey Mouse, and all the other beautiful tales.

All the seemingly 'terrible' things that had happened – rejection by the studios, the poverty, the filthy basement, the loneliness, were leading him directly to his destiny. He had a dream, talent, and discipline, but if things had gone the way he planned he'd have become just another employee and the world would never have been moved and inspired by his creations.

We are all the same – everything that happens to us is a vital part of the unfolding of our destiny, and there are no mistakes on that path. Imagine what a difference it would make if you knew that with unshakeable certainty, so that no matter what happened you didn't lose your dream. Everyone has a purpose, a mission and vision within, and the only difference between the masters and the masses is that the masses are distracted by the illusions of success and failure, gain and loss – the way things *look*, and the masters just hold the vision, no matter what happens, and see everything serving it. The masters just hold their vision *longer*, and that makes all the difference.

'Some things have to be seen to be believed.
Other things have to be believed to be seen.'
~ Anonymous ~

So it began, and years later when he was inspired to create Disneyland, it happened again. What he could see in his imagination had never existed before, so every bank he approached to borrow the money virtually laughed in his face, or shook their heads and advised him to give it up and stick to what he knew. In the end he had to go to 325 banks before he found one that was prepared to invest in him. 325! But he never gave up, because the vision and the voice on the inside were louder and clearer to him than all the voices on the outside. Every time he was rejected he simply used that experience to refine his proposal for the next bank, over and over and over again. Because of the clarity and power of his dream he didn't see failure, he merely saw a learning process, an education in the things he didn't know that were necessary to make it a reality.

If you don't buy into the illusions of success and failure along the path, if you stay true to your vision and inspired purpose and learn from everything that happens, nothing can stop you.

> *'There are no obstacles on the path.*
> *Obstacles ARE the path.'*
> ~ Zen Proverb ~

Jim Rohn said, 'To be successful, you should find out what failures did, and don't do it.' What all these extraordinary people have in common is a whole lot of challenges, and a refusal to give up. They had the strength and discipline to continue no matter what, and that's why we know them today. Real patience doesn't mean lying down on the job, or abdicating responsibility for your life by plodding along doing the bare minimum and being the victim of sharper operators. Did you know that if you owe $500 on a credit card, with 18.25% interest and a $40 annual fee, and you make the minimum payment every month, you'll owe $664 after 50 *years?!* That's not the kind of patience we're talking about, that's the stupidity of a sheep waiting to be shorn, and it will not take you where you want to go in life.

> *'If at first you don't succeed, try again, then give up.*
> *There's no use in being a damn fool about it.'*
> ~ W. C. Fields ~

He was joking, of course. Few people worked harder to escape terrible poverty than **W.C. Fields**, an orphan who lived alone in a hole in the ground and practiced juggling until his arms and legs were covered with blood and bruises. He later left America on a vaudeville tour and performed for the crowned heads of Europe before becoming one of the top movie stars of his era.

If you want to grow faster, don't do it by looking for luck or big gambles, increase your discipline! Instead of staying at the 10% savings we recommended, raise it by 10% every quarter and watch what happens. If you're saving $1000 per month, in three months it will be $1100, in another three months $1210, then $1320, $1450, $1600, $1760, $1940, $2140, $2350… It just keeps going up, and it *accelerates*. If quarterly seems too much, then do it twice a year, or once a year – the results will amaze you.

No one can stop you but you, and no one can save you but you, and that is perfect. When wealth arrives you won't owe anybody anything, you'll trust and respect yourself more than ever before, and you'll know that you *deserve* it, so you'll get to keep it.

We'll end this story-filled chapter with one more.

It is said that once there was a very holy man, who as a reward for his great virtue was taken up by the angels to visit heaven. They led him through heavenly mansions filled with rare, beautiful, and costly things, but as they passed through yet another great hall he noticed a huge room off to one side filled to its lofty ceiling with exquisitely wrapped gifts of every kind. He paused and asked his guides what they could possibly be, and they replied, "Oh, those are the gifts that people prayed for, but stopped praying just before they were to be delivered."

Prayer alone may not do it for you, because God helps those who help themselves, but consistency, discipline, and patience will. Don't ever give up. We've tried to illustrate the power of patience in this chapter but, like courage, it's not something you can give to someone, you can only help them discover it within themselves. The following exercise will remind you of the capacity you already have, and in the final chapter we'll reveal the most powerful way we know to not only increase it, but also how to attract more money into your life than ever before.

> *'Many of life's failures are people who did not realize how close they were to success when they gave up.'*
> ~ Thomas Edison ~

~ Exercise ~

Set aside some time when you know there will be no interruptions, and you're free to do a little inner time-travelling. Think back over your life, and remember three instances where you chose immediate gratification, the easy way out, or short-term gain. What were the results? What did it cost you? How lasting were the rewards? What did you lose? How did you feel afterwards?

Now think of three instances in your life when you went beyond what you thought you were capable of, where you were disciplined, deferred gratification, and truly committed yourself to achieving or mastering something. How did you feel when you finished? What benefits did you receive, and did they match the efforts you made? How did they contribute to and change you, and the course of your life?

With the passage of time and the benefit of hindsight, our choices become clear. We can view those episodes in their totality – beginning, middle, and end – and only then can we appreciate their true value, or lack of it. Use these insights into your past to encourage your will and help you create the future you would love to have.

'You cannot teach a man anything;
you can only help him to find it within himself.'
~ Galileo Galilei ~

Chapter 8

The Power of Purpose
Why Are You Here?

*'What our deepest self craves is not mere enjoyment,
but some supreme purpose that will enlist all our powers
and give unity and direction to our life.'*
~ Henry J. Golding ~

Well, here we are! You have followed the way of wealth to the final and most important chapter, the one which brings together and gives a deeper meaning to all the others. In Chapter 1 we talked about how voids create values, and the greater the void the greater the value, therefore the more energy and commitment you have to fulfil it. But the greatest void of all is the question human beings have asked themselves since the dawn of time – *Why am I here?* The answer to that question is your greatest value, and motivation, and power, and it can be summed up in one word – Purpose.

Have you ever wondered why so many scientists, writers, painters, musicians, philosophers, and teachers are so honoured, and live to such a great age? What they all have in common is an inspiring purpose, something that calls them to rise up every morning and create something new in the world, something beyond themselves that they feel inspired to participate in. It's no coincidence that people with a great purpose in life have *more* life – it's the law of supply and demand again, and those who make great demands on themselves are given more life and resources to fulfil their goals.

We've given you many 'sevens' so far, and here is the second last. There are 7 worldly powers, attributes that the world admires and rewards, and they are: intelligence, beauty, strength, wealth, social network (how many people you know and how many know you), will, and inspired purpose. The great secret is that simply by mastering the last of them, *purpose*, you can have all the others. That is the essence of this chapter, and in fact of this whole book. You may think, *My god, it's hard enough just surviving, let alone saving, and now you want me to find a purpose that will take more time and money?* Yes, we do, and here's why.

'He who has a big enough 'why' can bear any 'how.'
~ Friedrich Nietszche ~

How does purpose help you achieve the 7 powers? We'll use a story from a real life (because this has happened to some) to reveal its power. If you were to ask a stranger on the street for $5 for a cup of coffee, they would most likely either ignore you, or say 'no' and walk away. You'd have been embarrassed to ask, and humiliated or angry at the brush-off – lots of emotions, which we've seen are disempowering. But what if you were with your little son or daughter, had forgotten your wallet or simply had no money left, and they were crying with hunger? You'd be much more motivated to approach someone, they'd be much more likely to give, and although you may be a little embarrassed to ask, you'd both feel better about yourselves.

Now imagine that you wanted to feed all the homeless or hungry children in your city. Would you be ashamed to ask for a donation? No, you'd approach people with certainty because you were asking not just for yourself or your own family, but for a greater purpose. You'd be confident enough to go door-to-door and to local businesses, that energy would empower you, and many more people would give considerably more money to a bigger cause.

And if you decided that you wanted to help not just your city but hungry children all over your country – the poor, the homeless, single parent families in distress, native peoples, *all* of them – how motivated would you be then? You'd magnetically attract like-minded people to help you raise funds, as you grew you'd be interviewed by newspaper and radio journalists which would spread the word even faster and further, and more money would flow to you from not just local bodies but major companies as well.

And what if you then decided it wasn't enough just to help your own country, but the whole *planet*, and you set out to provide food, clothing, medical care, and education to children all over the world? How energised and focused and purposeful would you be then, and how much more powerful and magnetic would your message be? If you really committed yourself, you'd eventually appear on national and international television and other media, you'd approach and be approached by multi-national corporations, aid agencies, and even governments. Because you had a cause that was so far beyond your self, you'd *forget* yourself, and it would transform you. In devoting your whole being to something greater than you, you would discover in yourself will, intelligence, and strength, attract vast sums of money, and create a world-wide network... all from your inspired purpose. That's six of the seven powers. And, most unexpectedly, others would begin to recognise a beauty in you that you cannot see in yourself.

> *'If you help enough people get where they want to get in life,*
> *you'll get where you want to get in life.'*
> ~ Zig Ziglar ~

Why has 'The Wizard of Oz' been such an enduring classic in the hearts and minds of millions since it was released in 1939? Because purpose and love are its hidden message. The Scarecrow sought intelligence above all else, the Tin Man a heart, the Cowardly Lion courage, and Dorothy longed for home. By forgetting themselves in their love and care for her, they not only all found their heart's desire, they realised they'd always had it, just as she'd always had the power to go home within herself. They were simply unable to manifest it until each found a cause bigger than themselves, until they loved enough.

Being deeply loved by someone gives you strength,
While loving someone deeply gives you courage.'
~ Lao Tzu ~

We've used children to illustrate our point, but purpose can be anything that has meaning for you, touches you; building a business, creating an invention, writing a book, whatever inspires you. To the degree you fulfil the world's values, great wealth will flow to you, so make sure you link your purpose to the greatest possible benefit for the greatest number of people. Ask any group how many of them use 'Microsoft Windows', and you'll understand why Bill Gates is a billionaire. His genius produced something that *everybody* wanted, and his rewards are in exact proportion. It may seem like a paradox, but in order to receive more for yourself, at some point you're going to have to go *beyond* yourself. The universe doesn't misdirect its resources – the size of your purpose determines the amount of money that flows to it, and to you. This is the heart of our last truth.

'With what you get from others,
you make a living for yourself.
What you give to others,
makes a life for yourself.'
~ Hindu maxim ~

Financial & Universal Truth ~ 7 ~
Purpose is the Seed of Greatness

One day in 1974 a successful Bangladeshi businessman, Professor Muhammad Yunus, was walking through a village when he saw a line of men carrying everything from a tiny mud hut and piling it on a horse-drawn wagon, leaving not a plate or spoon or shirt inside. A ragged woman was huddled outside the hut, crying, and he stopped to ask her what was happening. He was shocked to learn that she had missed a single payment to a moneylender, so he was legally confiscating everything she owned, and that this was common in her village.

Appalled at such injustice he inquired further, and found that when very poor people wanted to start a small business, the banks would have nothing to do with them, so they were forced to resort to usurious money-lenders who not only charged up to 2,000% interest, but also made borrowers sell their product to the lender for whatever he chose to pay, which was of course so little that it was impossible for them to ever get out of debt. He then went through the entire village and found others in the same situation. The total of 42 people, who'd lost or were about to lose what little they had, were having their lives ruined by a combined debt of $27.

He paid it all with money from his pocket, and the villagers were in tears, clustering round to thank him and touch his sleeve in gratitude. He was so moved at being able to do so much, for so many, for so little, that he decided to make it his mission to help others. He created a company called Grameen ('village bank' in Bengali), and he's now acknowledged as the inventor of micro-finance. The business specialised in lending to the poor at very low rates of interest, attracted investment from wealthy individuals and companies throughout the sub-continent, and has since loaned nearly $11 billion. Even more extraordinary is the fact that there are no written contracts, every loan is based entirely on trust, and the repayment rate is an unbelievable 97%.

He was already successful, but he would never have been able to raise $11 billion without a cause that was much bigger than himself – purpose led him to achievements beyond his imagination. Purpose is the greatest power of all, and has the opposite effect of winning a lottery. It's like throwing 'Miracle-Gro' on your *spirit*, and your 'character defects' just wither away when you stop feeding them with your attention.

'When you are inspired by some great purpose,
all your thoughts break their bonds,
your mind transcends limitations and
your consciousness expands in all directions.
Dormant forces, faculties and talents become alive,
and you discover yourself to be a
greater person by far than you ever dreamed yourself to be.'
~ Patanjali ~

The greater your service to the world, the greater your reward and the bigger the game you get to play in, but you won't know that until you begin. Those we remember for their achievements and gifts to the world didn't know they could do it until they did it – so who is to say *you're* not the one to make a tremendous difference in the world? Certainly not you, because if you're honest you'll realise that you don't really know *who* you are, *where* you came from, where you're *going*, nor why you're *here*. And certainly not others; they not only don't know you, they're seeing you through their own illusions and voids. Anyone who believes they're too small to make a difference never spent a night with a mosquito.

We're all plagued by fears and doubts, they make us lose faith in ourselves, sap our heart and energy, but you are more than you know. That's why you need a big cause in your life, because until your motivation is greater than your fears and inertia, you'll stay small; you will achieve in proportion to that ratio. FIND YOUR PURPOSE – it will deliver you from a life of quiet desperation and open vast doors that would otherwise remain closed to you.

> *'Our doubts are traitors,*
> *and make us lose the good we oft might win,*
> *by fearing to attempt.'*
> ~ William Shakespeare ~

Tim ~ Part IV

A few years ago I met a friend for breakfast in a local café, and as we talked it became clear that beneath the light conversation he was anything but relaxed. I asked him what was going on, and he suddenly became serious. He said he felt that he'd come to a crossroads in his life; he knew what he wanted to do, that he felt called and inspired to do it, but he was afraid to take the next step. It was obviously deeply important to him, so we walked to a nearby park, sat down on a bench beneath some trees overlooking the harbour, and had the following conversation that changed his life.

He said, 'I've always loved business, and I'm very good at it, but it's just not enough for me anymore. What I'd really love to do is become a public speaker and teach people about universal principles, but I'd feel like a fraud teaching something I haven't yet mastered.'

I replied, 'Well, mastery is a very relative term, and actually it's a path with no end. But fear like that is usually based on comparing ourselves to others, so mastery in relation to whom?'

'Umm, I guess Dr Demartini, and you.'

'And who are you already masterful compared to?'

'Well, the public don't know this information, so I guess my audience.'

'And who else?'

'Come to think of it, most of the people I know and interact with.'

'So you already have a degree of relative mastery, right?'

'Hmm ... it feels funny to say so, but yes, I guess I do.'

We only stop ourselves from having or doing what we'd love when the obstacles seem greater than the benefits and possibilities, so I started balancing them out with him. 'Good. And what would be the drawbacks of waiting until you felt like a master before acting?'

'Well, that would take a long time and I want to speak now – I love it. All the people I could share this with will be forced to wait and won't have it to expand their lives, just because I'm afraid, and I don't want my fear to deprive anyone of this amazing wisdom. And I'd be missing out on the money I could make doing it.'

'Great, what else?'

'The more I learn the more I realise I don't know, so I'll probably never feel like a master and wouldn't ever do it. And of lot of it is so complex that it goes right over my head, so maybe my level of understanding could make it simpler and clearer for them.'

'So is it your humility or your pride that's holding you back?'

'Ha! I thought it was my humble sincerity, but it's actually my pride. That feels very different.'

Then I asked him, 'And what would be the benefits of acting sooner rather than later?'

'Well, I'd get the feedback and refinement that comes with presenting new material – their questions would tell me their values and what to *focus on to teach it better. Also, I'd have the pressure of the commitment making me study and practice and learn faster. And I'd get paid to do what I love, and that always stimulates me to grow.'*

'And how else would it benefit you to start now?'

He closed his eyes for a few moments, thinking deeply, and then said, 'I never realised this until now, but I know more about universal principles than most people, and what I've learned has been priceless to me, so it will probably be the same for them. I'll find out that I know more than I think I know when they appreciate it.'

'And how will not knowing it all help you?'

'What?! Oh, right, you mean that everything serves. Well, thinking I'm not good enough would keep me from getting cocky so I won't need to be put down by the audience, or the world.'

'That's true. So what would be the drawbacks of presenting as an absolute master?"

'You're kidding, right? There wouldn't be any drawbacks, it would be fantastic!'

'You know everything has two sides in order to exist — it's a dual universe. Look again.'

'Well, maybe it would take so long and I'd become so centred that I'd forget what it was like to be poor or afraid or off purpose, and I couldn't relate to them.'

'Good. And maybe you wouldn't care anymore?'

'What? What do you mean?'

'If you saw divine order and balance all around you, realised that everyone was having exactly the same proportion of pain and pleasure in their lives, and that they were all exactly where they needed to be to learn their next lesson, would you want to fix anything?'

He went absolutely still and quiet as that sank in, and didn't speak for two minutes, then said, slowly; 'My god, if I was a good as I think I should be to do this work, I wouldn't see any need to do it! I'd go on to the next thing, wouldn't I? So it's actually my so-called imperfection that's making me 'perfect' to do it right now?'

'Exactly. You understand peoples' fears because you share them, and you know their obstacles because you have them too. You're concerned

about not knowing enough, so you'll stay humble. There's an old Zen saying, "In the beginner's mind there are many possibilities, in the expert's mind there are few." You have an open beginner's mind, which has tremendous potential. You really care about people because you're trying to rescue parts of yourself. You'll be paid while you're learning, and having to teach it will accelerate the process. That's all great stuff, and true. So what's in the way of you speaking right now?'

'I just thought I had to be a genius, and I'm not.'

'Real genius has nothing to do with IQ. It comes from the Latin root 'to shine' and a genius is simply anyone who listens to the light of their own spirit and obeys.'

'Well, I know I can do that.'

'And isn't that what people really want to hear anyway, their inner soul's message of certainty rather than their outer mind's doubts? Did you know that one of the big drawbacks to having a high IQ is that it can come with a big ego which won't acknowledge any higher authority? Their pride can cut them off from their higher self. Would you give up your connection with spirit to be smarter?'

'No way! That's what makes me a great speaker, that I can talk from my heart, not my head. I don't care so much about all the other stuff.'

He almost had it now, so I then asked him; 'Have you ever met your fantasy of a 'perfect' human?'

'No, I guess not.'

'So if you were perfect the way you fantasised, would you even be a real person? Isn't having something to reach for and grow towards vital for the human spirit?'

'Yes, it is.'

I know that when we take the time to listen, the inner voice always speaks to us, so I then asked him; 'So what is the light of your soul telling you about this?'

He got present then, was silent for a minute, and tears came to his eyes; 'To speak, and it will speak through me. I can have a script, but the real talk will come spontaneously from my heart when I let go.'

'So if you heard that, you must be a genius.'

'I guess I must be. And a genius who isn't afraid to be imperfect *according to a fantasy, but perfect according to the truth of human nature...'*

'Is a perfect genius. Accepting yourself exactly as you are, with all your qualities, gives you the courage to do what you feel called to do. Einstein said that if God is omniscient and omnipresent then every human thought, word, and deed must also be His work. Isn't that what you want to teach people, that they have infinite potential just as they are?'

'Absolutely, and every time I stand on stage and admit that I'm afraid, or don't have the answers, I get more courage and more answers, and people really relate to me.'

'So what do you want to tell them?'

'That they're perfect just the way they are, that they have greatness within them, and their job here on earth is to express it.'

'So who's perfectly qualified to teach that, a so-called 'perfect' master, or a human being mastering the art by learning it himself?'

He laughed out loud then and said, 'I just saw how funny it would be to try to teach people to face their fears when I couldn't, pretending that I knew it all and trying to hide my doubts.'

'And can you see how your fear has led to this insight and increased your courage?'

'Yes, you're right, it has!'

'So you were never really off track, were you? Everything serves, and you're actually ready to act on your dream right now.'

'That's amazing. I'm perfectly imperfect and right on track, no matter what I think. Thank you so much,' and he gave me a big hug.

I then helped him see how he was already sharing that wisdom right now with his friends and children and employees, and we went through some action steps so he could start that day; studying, deciding how long he wanted to talk, when and where and to whom, and he was off and running. We are never given an idea or inspiration we can't act upon right now, at some level, and then keep growing from there.

Today that man stands on stage three times a week in front of large audiences, and speaks from his heart on wealth creation and universal principles. He's still a friend of mine, and his name is John Hanna.

'Our opinion of ourselves, like our shadow,
makes us either too big or too little.'
~ Benjamin Franklin ~

There are three human motivating forces, and the one you choose determines the quality of your life. One is avoiding pain, and for some people that's the most important thing in life. Another is seeking pleasure, and many live for it alone. But they're not only ultimately unfulfilling, they are impossible, for you'll always get both pain and pleasure no matter what you do. And neither will give you your purpose because their vision is too small; when life gets tough they give up – they won't pay the price of greatness.

The third motivator is inspiration, and it comes from some great purpose that makes all our self-imposed limitations disappear like mist in the rising sun. Professional athletes know that they risk physical injury and a possible lifetime of pain, but they do it gladly – because it is what they love to do, they pay the price. Inspiration knows the costs and the challenges, and does it anyway. When you're inspired, you embrace both pain *and* pleasure in the pursuit of your purpose, and you find fulfilment that is beyond either. Don't play small – give yourself permission to do something extraordinary with your life.

'Forget about likes and dislikes, they are of no consequence.
Just do what must be done.
This may not be happiness, but it is greatness.'
~ George Bernard Shaw ~

Will Smith is one of the most successful people in the world; first a recording artist, then a TV star, movie star, and now co-owner of a film production company with his wife Jada, he is a multi-millionaire and founder of philanthropic foundations for the young and underprivileged. When asked the secret of his success, he said, "Just an incredible work ethic," and then told this story. When he was a teenager, his father demolished the 12-foot-high, 60-foot-long stone wall in front of his business and told Will and his brother to rebuild it. They thought he was joking, and when they realised he was serious they whined and complained that it was impossible, but he insisted, so they began. It took them a year. On the day they finally finished he arrived at work, took one look at the wall, and said, "Now don't you *ever* tell me you can't do anything again," and went inside.

He relied on his father's will to get through that 'impossible' challenge, but afterwards he no longer doubted he could do impossible things, so he did them, one after another. What he thought so harsh in his father he eventually realised was great love and wisdom, and an extraordinary life was the result. Will Smith's father freed him from his own limitations, and once he stopped believing in them they lost all power over him. A sense of purpose will not only draw wealth to you, it can carry you through obstacles and challenges that would otherwise stop you in your tracks. The more you challenge *yourself*, the more you face your fears and discipline the part of you that just wants life small and easy, the more you'll do, and have, and become.

> *'All our dreams can come true,*
> *if we have the courage to pursue them.'*
> ~ Walt Disney ~

And it's not just philosophical, there is a very practical reason to bring vision and purpose to your wealth creation. Imagine that you're poor (not a big stretch for many of us), so poor that you have only $1 to your name. If someone then gives you another dollar, that new dollar has 100% value for you because it doubled your wealth, and you're very grateful for it. But if you have $100, the next dollar only has 1% value in terms of your net worth, and you're that much less grateful. If you have $1,000,000 another $1 or $100 or $1000 means almost nothing, and gaining or losing what meant so much to you becomes insignificant.

Now, here's the point. Remember we said that the greatest determinant of wealth is the strong desire to have it, and that most people are run by pain and pleasure? Well, every wealthy person, no matter how poor they begin, will eventually reach a point where they're no longer motivated by, or interested in, making more money. When the pleasure of what you have outweighs the painful memories of having nothing, or the pleasure of getting more becomes less than the pain/effort of making it, you'll lose your motivation and desire for more. At that exact moment you'll go off track and stop doing the things that made you wealthy; money will stop flowing *to* you and begin flowing *away* from you, to those who desire it more.

You can actually *graph* this phenomenon, with the vertical axis being desire and the horizontal axis wealth. You start out with very high desire and very low wealth, and at the point where the rising dollar line crosses the falling desire line, financial growth stops. The only solution is to make sure that your purpose grows with your wealth, that your reach always exceeds your grasp. As long as you have a purpose for money that's greater than what you have, you'll continue to increase in wealth. A strong and inspiring purpose will not only give you the drive to create wealth, later on it will keep you growing when others have fallen by the wayside.

So it's important to find your purpose, and don't waste even a moment thinking you don't have one, or don't care. We're all born innately knowing our purpose, what Napoleon Hill called the 'chief aim for life'. It's why you came here in the first place, but if that's so, why haven't you been living it right from the start? It's an odd thing, but we are not taught about two of the most important things in life – love and money. It's simply assumed we know how to love, and for most of us it takes a lifetime of trial and error and heartbreak to finally learn. Neither are we taught about finance, which is why so many become wage-slaves, and it's the same with purpose; parents spend far more time teaching their children how to brush their teeth than how to find their purpose.

But imagine if your parents had asked you this from a very early age – not just; "What are you going to be when you grow up?" but, "What is your purpose here, my darling? What would you love to do in life? What is your gift to the world?"

It would be impossible not to have a completely different life, because the quality of your life is determined by the quality of the questions you ask. High quality questions create a high quality life, and these are questions of the very highest quality. Without a meaning and a point for life you don't have much love or gratitude for life – in fact, you don't have much *life*.

Why do you think the death statistics accelerate right off the chart 18-24 months after retirement? Because after a lifetime of productive work people suddenly have no purpose to live, and no will to live is a will to die. Have you ever known someone who was suicidal? They always say, "What's the point?" They give up on life because it all seems meaningless and they can see no *purpose* to existence. You achieve maximum potential from your life when you have clarity of purpose.

If you think you don't know your purpose, or perhaps fear to admit it even to yourself, here's a way to get in touch with it. *If you knew you couldn't fail,* if the outcome was guaranteed by some omnipotent being, what would you love to do with your life? The answer to that question is the path to your purpose.

> **'Your work is to discover your work,**
> **and then with all your heart give yourself to it.'**
> ~ The Buddha ~

There was a young woman who loved to write, and every free moment from her job teaching primary school and caring for her own children, she'd immerse herself in the world of her imagination. Nothing she wrote was ever published, she never made a penny from it and collected a huge pile of editors' rejection slips, but she persisted because it was what she loved. Even after her marriage ended, and she lost her job, when she was an unemployed single mother trying to raise her family, she went on writing.

Then one day she boarded a train, and as she sat down she heard a voice in her head say clearly, "There was a young boy who was a wizard, but didn't know it." That was all it said, but by the end of the journey she knew the boy's name, the name of his school and some of his teachers, the challenges he would face, who his friends and enemies would be, and she couldn't wait to get home and put it down on paper.

A documentary was made of her life many years later, after success beyond anything she'd ever imagined, and they took her to the little flat she'd been living in at the time. She hadn't been back since, and when she stepped into the room she began to cry, and said, "This is where it all began. Life was so hard and I had no idea how we were going to survive. I just wrote the books because I had to, there was something inside that wanted to come out. I am so grateful to that young woman that I was, for her courage and determination – it's as if she was somebody else, but she gave me everything."

Without the powerful sense of purpose that sustained her through the challenges and poverty and fears, J. K. Rowling would never have become the wealthiest and most successful writer the world has ever known, and billions would never have been touched, delighted, and inspired by Harry Potter. A poor young woman alone in a rented flat changed the world because she listened to the voice inside, had the discipline to follow it, and refused to give up.

'Nothing is Impossible'
Chiselled into the entrance floor at
~ Saatchi & Saatchi ~

We said that when you're truly committed, metaphysics also comes to help you. Well, J. K. Rowling is not alone in having something very like magic come to the aid of purpose.

Back in the 1960s, John Phillips was a young musician with a fine ear for harmony who was putting together a band. He found a beautiful girl with a clear soprano (later Michelle Phillips), and a guitarist who could sing (Denny Doherty), but he needed a fourth voice. Michelle had a very overweight friend who'd dreamed all her life of being a famous singer, and she begged to be allowed to audition. Phillips didn't like her looks, but grudgingly allowed her to try out before rejecting her because her voice was half an octave too high. But no one else appeared who could even sing well enough, let alone harmonise, so he let her practice with them. She felt this was her destiny, that it was meant to be, so she endured his mockery and abuse.

When the band went to the Caribbean to rehearse she had to pay for her own airfare and accommodation, so she borrowed the money. A week later Phillips snapped, shouting at her to go home because she ruined his

*harmonies, and just at that moment a heavy stage light fell from high
above onto her head. Dazed and bloody, she staggered outside to sit on the
beach, crying in disbelief that her life-long dream was broken, then passed
out. She eventually woke up and, still groggy, wandered back into the
studio and began to sing along. Phillips glared at her, then stared at her,
then stopped her. To his amazement her voice had dropped exactly half an
octave, and the harmonies were perfect. It was impossible, but it happened.*

She was in, 'The Mamas and The Papas' were complete, and Cass
Elliot began her career in one of the most successful bands of the era,
just as she'd always known in her heart. Don't underestimate the power
of the human spirit to affect physical reality. Only a dream and sense of
purpose sustained her, then drew in the 'accident' that changed her voice
to harmonise perfectly with where she was determined to be.

> *'You are never given a wish or an idea
> without also being given the power to make it come true.
> But you may have to work for it.'*
> ~ Richard Bach ~
> author of 'Jonathan Livingstone Seagull'

Sometimes we feel sorry for ourselves and believe we can't possibly
do anything exceptional until things get better, some problem is resolved,
or we 'feel ready'. This is another illusion that can rob us of precious time,
and you've learned how vital a factor time is in wealth creation. Dr John F.
Demartini is committed to making a difference for millions of desperately
poor Africans, and presents seminars there to help them help themselves.
On one of his visits he was introduced to a young man who was living the
principles as very few have, and John speaks of him around the world to
those who believe their path is too hard.

*He is a 14 year-old African boy with almost no education. As is all
too common there, both his parents had died of AIDS, so as the eld-
est he became the sole parent and provider for his nine brothers and
sisters. They all live together in a dirt-floored tin shack 8 ½ feet by 10*

feet, without electricity or water. He walks for an hour every morning to board a truck that drives him and other labourers for two hours, then walks another hour to his job, works a back-breaking eight hours and then reverses his journey every night, and for this he earns $200 a year. His dream is to save $20 a year (he had saved $7 in the first quarter) to buy a bigger shack with one electric wire, for $200.

*Most people would give up in such circumstances and surrender to despair, but not him. Far from being depressed or bitter, he is confident, enthusiastic, fulfilled, and determined to teach 1000 other children to do what he's done, and free themselves from poverty. He has a **purpose**, and it gives him the heart to not only save his family, but inspire countless others in Africa and all over the world. Thanks to a powerful purpose life cannot grind him down, it is polishing him into a diamond, and he shines brightly in the darkness.*

> ### 'Champions aren't made in the gym.
> ### They're made from a vision, a dream, a purpose,
> ### something deep inside them.'
> ~ Muhammad Ali ~

There are three basic types of human beings in the world:
1. Those who gossip about other people.
2. Those who complain about their own problems.
3. Those who talk about and focus on their dreams.

You determine who you are by what you say, and any time or energy you spend judging yourself or others is taken from your creative capacity to build a magnificent life. Your thoughts and words are important, and so are the people you associate with. If you associate with the first two types, the small-visioned people, they'll try to pull you down to their level. But if you associate with the third type, those with vision, they'll lift you *up* to theirs – choose to fly with the eagles, not the turkeys, because birds of a feather do flock together.

In 1997, Jack Canfield, co-author of the bestseller 'Chicken Soup for the Soul', read an extraordinary article in a newspaper. In Tallahassee, Florida, Laura Shultz heard screaming in her front driveway and ran from the house to find her teenage grandson being crushed beneath the axle of his car after the jack collapsed. Without pausing to think, the 63-year-old, 100 lb. grandmother raced over and lifted the entire back end of the heavy Buick by herself, allowing bystanders to pull him free. The ambulance arrived, the boy survived, and when neighbours asked how she did it, she didn't know what they were talking about. She could barely remember her impossible feat of strength, only aware that she'd had to save her grandson.

Jack was so impressed that he called Laura to speak with her about the miracle, and was surprised to be greeted with a cold, "I do not want to talk about that incident," before she hung up. Thinking he'd been mis-understood he called back and said, "Laura, this is Jack Canfield again, I interview Olympic athletes and top performers…"only to be interrupted with the same answer and another sharp click as the receiver went down.

Many months passed, Jack found himself giving a seminar in Tallahassee, and he took time out to drive to Laura's house in another attempt to interview her. He knocked on the door and introduced him-self, Laura said, "I know who you are, young man," and with old-school southern courtesy invited him in for a cup of coffee. He made small talk while they drank, but every time he tried to turn the conversation to that day she would simply change the subject.

Finally he said, "Laura, I get that you don't want to talk about it, but what I don't understand is **why**."

She looked down at her cup for a moment, then seemed to gather herself, raised her head and spoke passionately; "Because that day I did something **impossible**, and ever since I've been asking myself, 'Have I wasted my life?'"

Jack was astonished and stammered, "But, but… what you did was amazing! You should be proud!"

"Well, I'm not. I did something I never thought I could do, and now not a day goes by that I don't look back on my life and wonder just how many other things I could have done, but never even tried because I thought I couldn't. I have no idea what's possible and what isn't any-more, and now I can't stop thinking, **Have I wasted my life?**"

Don't let it happen to you. Don't wait to be crushed beneath a heavy burden, or by the weight of years, before realising you could have done more. We regret the things we *didn't* do so much more than anything we actually do. Stand on Laura's shoulders and realise that you can't know what you're capable of until you try. Find something you care about as much as she did her grandson, and amaze yourself at what you can accomplish. Place a great demand on yourself, and watch the supply appear – a *cause* beyond yourself gives you *strength* beyond yourself.

> ### 'Only those who risk going too far can possibly find out how far one can go.'
> ~ T.S. Eliot ~

So, a sad story? Not at all. Jack was so impressed by Laura's honesty and courageous ability to face her own fears that they spoke for hours that day, and he stayed in touch, helping her to find the hidden opportunity in her crisis. He was an eagle, not a turkey, and he helped her rise to his level. Today Laura Shultz is a highly successful motivational speaker who travels across America sharing her story, helping thousands break through their limitations to find a bigger purpose in life. Even 63 years of timidity was not a mistake, it's what gave her the drive to do so much when her time finally came. Because she did less than she might have then, she's doing more than she ever imagined now – from her smallness came greatness.

Tiny atoms, of which we and everything else in the universe is made, are 99.9999% *empty space*, yet look what they can become. Do you think you're any less worthy than an atom? You have vast untapped resources within you. After World War II, Albert Einstein became Professor in Residence at the Institute for Advanced Studies in Princeton. One day a visitor asked to see the great man's laboratory where he made his world-shaking discoveries. Albert just smiled, lifted his fountain pen, and pointed to his head. Think of this when you doubt your own capacity, and remember that Disney is a $70 billion empire started by... a mouse.

The Chinese character for wealth is composed of two symbols;
a seashell – an ancient form of currency,
and another – 'the unique talent or ability we each possess'.
The literal meaning is 'brilliance'.

Purpose may seem challenging, but it's so much easier than the alternative, which is life without purpose, and the inner and outer rewards can be immense. Here's what is possible for those who find what they love, and then do it:

When Microsoft shares split in 1995, **Bill Gates** doubled his fortune to $55 billion. That's about $1 billion a week, or $150 million a day, $6 million per hour, $1 million every 10 minutes, $100,000 a minute, or $1,666 a second, every second of every day of the year. He said recently, "I do have a big responsibility – how to give the money back," and he's become the greatest philanthropist the world has ever known, donating more than twice as much anyone else on record.

J.K. Rowling earns $192 every minute of the year.

Paris Hilton charges $650,000 just to attend a party.

Rod Stewart receives $22,000 a minute for his appearances.

George Michael made almost $4 million per hour when he performed at a New Year's Eve party in Russia in 2006.

Ray Evans (1915-2007) co-wrote the Christmas carol 'Silver Bells' in two days, in 1951. To the end of his life he received $600,000 every year in royalties from that one song.

Nolan Bushell founded Atari with $500. Four years later he sold it to Warner for $28 million.

The inventors of 'YouTube' received $11.5 million in start-up capital in late 2005, early 2006. Google bought them out in November 2006 for $1.61 billion.

Paul McCartney woke up one morning having dreamed a song. He went to the piano and began picking it out, but had no lyrics so he sang 'scrambled eggs' because it fit the meter. It took him about half an hour, and 'Yesterday' became the most recorded song in history. It has been estimated that it's being played somewhere in the world every minute of the day, and the royalties are stupendous.

Elton John's fee is $4 million for a private performance, but he's also famous for his generosity. His manager, John Reed, took him to lunch one day, and they dropped in at a Rolls-Royce showroom on the way home. Selecting a new limousine for each of them, Elton said, "I'll get these, you got lunch." He also bought Reed a yacht and a helicopter – that year.

Don Maclean wrote the huge hit 'American Pie' that everyone loved but no one understood. He was constantly being asked what the lyrics meant, but was smart enough not to spoil the mystery. One day he looked the ten-thousandth interviewer in the eye and said, 'It means I never have to work again as long as I live.'

> ### 'Find out what you love to do,
> ### and you'll never work a day in your life.'
> ~ Thomas Edison ~

All of these people gave the world something that it wanted, and they received fabulous rewards for their gifts. Like anyone, they had to work for their achievements, they faced their fears and challenges along the way, but none of them would say it wasn't worth it because it freed them to do what they love.

Do what you love. It's hard enough to be here as it is, and every day you fill with things you don't love reduces your life force. Now do you understand why saving is at the heart of our advice to you? When you find your purpose, you want to be able to follow wherever it leads. With financial independence you won't squander your precious life on a meaningless job that drains you, but be free to dedicate it to an inspiring purpose that gives back far more than it ever takes.

Now, a cynic could say that this is all wishful thinking and pixie dust, that almost no one ever makes this magical transformation, and they'd be right … but statistics lie. Yes, only a tiny percentage of humanity achieves true greatness, but of those with a vision and purpose and *never give up on it*, 100% succeed. Listen to the inner voice of certainty, not the outer voices of doubt, and you will be one of the great ones.

> ### 'Every creation is a victory over fear.'
> ~ Francis Ford Coppola ~

We said way back in Chapter 1 that the most important single factor in wealth creation is a strong desire to possess it, and that's true, but there is one more factor that is equally important – in order to receive it you must also believe that you *deserve* wealth. The greater your achievements and gifts to the world, the more certain you'll be that you truly deserve wealth, and it will flow to you.

Whatever your talent, your dream, your mission or cause or purpose in life – find it, grow it, *live* it. When you do, you'll understand that nothing was ever able to stop you but you. Don't settle for a life of half-fillment when genuine fulfillment is not only available to you, it's your destiny.

'We have met the enemy, and they are us.'
~ Pogo ~

We want to leave you with one more tale, a very old parable from the Bible. Like fables, parables are hidden wisdom in story form.

A master summoned his three servants, and gave them each a gift; to the first servant he gave five talents (an ancient weight measure) of silver, to the second two talents, and to the last one talent. Then he left them in charge of his house and went on a long journey. Upon his return he called them all before him again and asked how their talents had fared.

The first servant said, "Lord, you gave me five talents, and here I have gained five talents more," and the master replied, "Thou good and faithful servant, you have been faithful over a few things, so I will make you ruler over many things."

The second servant stepped forward to say that he also had turned his two talents into two more, and the master praised him in exactly the same way. But the third servant was ashamed and said, "Lord, I was afraid to lose what you gave me, so I buried it in the earth. There is the talent, still safe."

His master then frowned upon him and said, "Thou unworthy servant, I gave so that you may increase it, but you have wasted my gift," and he commanded that the unworthy servant's talent be given to the one with ten talents.

To those who have, more is given; to those who have not, more is taken away. You too have been given gifts, unique talents and abilities, and it's your responsibility to make the most of them, because no-one else is going to get up in the morning and dedicate themselves to transforming your life. If you choose not to, that's okay – many take that path. Just know that the wealth and fulfilment you could have achieved won't disappear, they will simply be given to those who *do* use their gifts. And when you find your gift, and connect it to your cause, remember the wisdom of a tiny but powerful Jedi master:

> ### 'Do, or do not. There is no 'try'.'
> ~ Yoda ~

An old and somewhat bitter joke says that you can tell what God thinks about money by looking at the people he gives it to. The implication is that it's a bad thing that only goes to bad people, and that's a myth, but there is truth hidden here. It's not about good or evil; money flows to those who truly desire it, who discipline themselves to master it, and who devote their lives to a purpose. That's all it takes, and if you apply what we've taught you, you'll find out just how true that is. That's the essence of our message, and now it's up to you. And remember, you will never be alone on this journey; the masters are with you in word and spirit, if you'll only listen, and the universe itself supports in unimaginable ways every genuine effort you'll ever make to fulfil your destiny and become your true self.

> *'There is one elementary truth, the ignorance of which*
> *kills countless ideas and splendid plans:*
> *the moment one definitely commits oneself,*
> *then Providence moves too.*
> *All sorts of things occur to help one*
> *that would never otherwise have occurred...*
> *Whatever you can do, or dream you can do, begin it.*
> *Boldness has genius, power, and magic in it.*
> *Begin it now.'*
> ~ Johann Wolfgang von Goethe ~

~ Exercise ~

A very few have been blessed with innate knowledge of their purpose from an early age, but for the vast majority who haven't (the rest of us), this simple exercise is incredibly effective in helping to awaken it. Again, the magic requires nothing but a pen and a piece of paper, and our final '7'.

Every morning, as soon as you're clear-headed, (if you're not a morning person, do it the night before) take a moment to write down the 7 highest priority actions you know you can do, *today*, that will help you fulfil your dreams and purpose. That means 7 things you're going to do this day that you *know* will have a beneficial effect on your life. Some will be challenging – the things you have fear or doubt about, and some will be supportive – the things you love. You want to make it a mixture of both; not just a list of onerous duties to threaten yourself with, but something that will inspire you into action.

For example, a typical list might be:
1. Meditate
2. Study
3. Write
4. See clients
5. Exercise
6. Clean the house
7. Go for a walk in nature

It may also be sort out your accounts, do your tax, dig the garden, deposit savings, update your investment pyramid, tell your spouse you love them (and mean it), read an inspiring book, work on your website, learn marketing, enrol in a seminar, and so on. Some things can't be completed in one day, and that's fine, the point is that you'll *start* them, and then continue. That's all very well, but how is this going to help you find your purpose?

First of all, procrastination is the thief of time, and this will help you transcend it. It's a very strange effect, but you'll find that the likelihood of your doing something is more than trebled by simply writing it down.

As long as we keep them in our heads, we can avoid things for days and weeks and months, but when you write something down it's as if you've made a promise to yourself, and you don't want to break it.

At first you may choose the easiest tasks, but eventually you'll find yourself doing the toughest ones too, because anything you don't do that day is automatically rolled over and written at the top of tomorrow's list. You can't avoid it, so you not only do it, you do it *first*, and you'll find that often most of the list is completed before midday – so it also creates discipline and courage. Date each list, and check items off as you complete them. There's a surprising satisfaction in this simple act, and it increases your sense of effectiveness and self-worth.

This exercise should become an integral part of your life because it will help you break intimidating tasks down into doable bite-size pieces. By the mile it's a pile, by the yard it's hard, but by the inch it's a cinch.

And finally, here's the core effect: after three months, go back over your list of dated priority actions, and you'll find three or four items appearing over and over again. When you do them your life flows and works, and when you don't, it doesn't. Whatever they are, these are the keys to your purpose, and you'll realise, "My god, that's my life course." This is the single most effective way we know to organise your day, focus your actions and intent, discover your purpose, and prioritise your life. Acting on priorities is vital because it maximises your productivity and achievement. This exercise will discipline you to act here and now with increased potential, and then in ever-greater time frames, tasks, and futures.

And… that's all we can do for you, for now. The choice is yours; to remain with the masses, or join the masters. Thank you for dedicating the time to read this book – now go out and live it. We wish you every success on your journey.

'Two roads diverged in a wood,
and I – I took the one less travelled by,
and that has made all the difference.'
~ Robert Frost ~

~ Epilogue ~

Well, that's all we wrote, folks. Our last story was from the Bible, which is fitting because it bears some relation to the final words we have to share with you. When it comes time for you to leave this earth, there will be a Day of Judgement, and a Question asked. The judgement will not be about salvation, because you were never lost, and the one who asks the question will be the one who answers it – *you*. Just as in life, no-one can judge you but you.

You're going to ask yourself; "Did I do everything I could with everything I was given?" and you'll want to be able to answer; "Yes, I did! I gave it everything I had, and I lived a magnificent life."

If you take to heart and apply everything we've spoken of here, that will be the truth, and you'll have nothing to judge yourself for. And please, do use our websites to let us know what you thought of the book, and how things are going for you. It would be nice to know how the starfish are doing.

~ John Hanna ~ Biography

John Hanna arrived in Australia at age 7 to find it was not such a lucky country for his family. A childhood of great poverty gave him the lifelong desire to master wealth – his father died penniless at the young age of 57, never having fulfilled his great dreams. This drive led John to not only create his own companies, but to study the works of all the leading experts on finance and living an empowered life. Finally discovering a field of metaphysics called Universal Principles, he found that his life began to change dramatically.

At the age of 34 he finally achieved his goal of becoming a millionaire, lost it all, then regained it again. Now he wants to help those with the same desire to be more, to make their dreams a reality.

John has dedicated his life to the study of these Universal Principles, particularly as they relate to the creation of wealth and the power of the mind. His desire is to travel the world sharing his knowledge and experience so that, unlike his father, people can live a life of purpose and fulfillment doing what they love and loving what they do, being not servants to money but masters of it.

john@johnhanna.com
www.johnhanna.com

~ Timothy Marlowe ~ Biography

Born in 1952, Tim has spent nearly 60 years searching for an answer to the question 'What the hell are we doing here?' – this book is the latest result of that quest. With over 30 different jobs by the age of 30, from funeral home and hospitality to yoga and meditation teacher, property sales, editor, and ghost writer, he has consistently sought knowledge for its own sake.

A deep study of Eastern philosophy and mysticism took him from Vipassana and the Wu Tao to 9 years with a Tibetan lama, coming full circle back to the West with the profound teachings of Dr. John F Demartini, with whom he has studied for the past 16 years and collaborated on several books.

Tim loves cycling, skiing, bushwalking and dogs. A voracious reader (3-5 books a week for 50 years), he is utterly reliant on his beautiful and talented wife Désirée to deal with any technology more complex than a bicycle. John Hanna is his dear and unlikely friend, without whom this book would not exist.

tim.marlowe@optusnet.com.au
www.demarlowe.com.au

The Cathedral

We thought we were done, the book was finished and edited, but that little voice kept whispering that there was something more, one final message. We've learned not to ignore it, and sure enough this story appeared in memory and would not go away. It reaches far beyond wealth and success, desirable as they are, and is our last gift to you.

Chartres Cathedral is one of the most magnificent examples of Gothic architecture in the world. Built on the principles of sacred geometry, this extraordinary creation was begun in 1193 and finished in 1250. When construction had been under way for 25 years, a traveller came from Italy on his grand tour of Europe to see the greatest works of man. Upon reaching the site he found a hive of activity, and seeing a man in a trench he asked him what he did there. The man merely grunted, "I dig the foundations," and kept on shovelling. Walking further he came across a worker covered in dust and asked him the same question; "I'm a stone mason. I build the walls, and we're too busy to talk here." The next man wore a leather apron and he answered; "I'm a carpenter. I build the scaffolding for the wall-builders to stand on," and hurried off.

The traveller was also a philosopher, and he marvelled to see such beauty created by simple labourers. Walking on, he left them all behind and eventually found an elderly woman with a broom, sweeping up rubbish in the heart of the cathedral shell. By now expecting the same kind of answer, he nevertheless asked her, "And what is it that you do here, my good woman?"

The woman stopped sweeping, gazed at the stone walls rising into the air around her, and said in a surprisingly clear voice, "What do I do here? I'm building a cathedral to the glory of almighty God." She looked the traveller in the eyes for a moment before going back to work, and he knew his question had been answered.

'What are you doing here?' It's a big question, possibly the greatest of all, and your answer will tell you why your life is as it is. Even though her physical work was the most lowly, that woman's state of mind was the highest – so profound that we still remember her almost 1000 years later. What if you had the same sense of value and power and connection to something higher in your own life? What might you achieve then? Find your dream, discover what means as much to you as her cathedral meant to that old woman, and not only will you live a magnificent and fulfilling life, they'll be talking about you a thousand years from now.

'If you don't know who you are,
how will the world recognise you?'
~ Timothy Marlowe ~

" 'Way of the Wealthy' is clear, informative, revealing, inspiring and filled with life-changing philosophical principles and practical financial action steps that can change personal and financial destinies."
~ Dr John F. Demartini ~
Founder of the Demartini Institute, author

" 'Way of the Wealthy' is quite simply wonder-full. I never expected to be touched and moved by a book on wealth creation, but it's so much more than that. The stories and quotes are truly inspirational, and the message of loving life and finding your purpose ring so true. This is a beautiful book for everyone."
~ Delta Goodrem ~ Singer/Songwriter

" I have very little spare time for reading, but this one was worth it. It spoke to me because I know what it takes to make a dream come true, and the courage, discipline, and heart are all here. Also, the great stories make it incredibly easy to read. 'Way of the Wealthy' is a real champion.' "
~ Kostya Tszyu ~
Four-time World Light Welterweight Champion

Have you ever wondered why some people seem to have so much, and others so little? What makes them different? There is a lot more to it than hard work, intelligence, or luck – and this fascinating book reveals why.

In a unique exploration of financial and universal laws through story, humour, profound insight, and powerful exercises, WoW clearly sets out how to not only create vast wealth, but even more importantly how to keep it, to grow it, and use it to build a magnificent life.

Be prepared for dramatic changes, for it will free you from old beliefs about what you deserve and why you're here. 'Way of the Wealthy' is not a book you read, but a book you live, and it will utterly transform your wealth and your life.

Printed in Australia
AUOC01n0820020517
285295AU00005B/5/P